Laure Far

15 FUN PROJECTS
to Add Decorating Charm to Your Home

PAPER JOY

FOR EVERY ROOM

SCHIFFER
PUBLISHING
4880 Lower Valley Road • Atglen, PA 19310

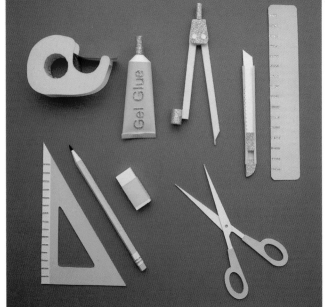

Laure's Secrets

The Kitchen

The Living Room

Baby's Bedroom

Parents' Bedroom

The Garden

" What if I decorated my home with paper? "

I have the pleasure, in the pages ahead, of helping you discover and share these 15 projects with a happiness as great as the joy that inspired and guided me.

Whether they also incorporate everyday objects or are 100% paper, the creations I share in these pages are decorations in their own right, and you'll learn that paper isn't synonymous with ephemeral. Divided into six colorful chapters, for each of the rooms in your house, the projects are easy to make, and their styles are just "reality"-based enough to blend in with your interior.

In this book, I also reveal some of my little secrets and show you around my own creation process. Plus we'll go over techniques and tips to help you work with paper more easily.

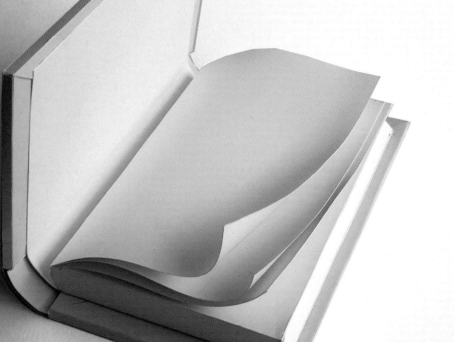

Ready, set
. . . start
cutting!

Who am I?

My name is Laure and *papier* papier PAPIER is my little business.

After studying art, I taught art for a while, but the desire to create was so strong that I started making paper scenes that I published on Instagram. In only a year, this creative activity of mine became a full-time job!

Paper offers us a multitude of possibilities, so it really drew me: a material that's fragile and solid, supple and rigid. I learned to master it.

Poetry, plausibility, and a bit of fun—that could perfectly describe all of my work.

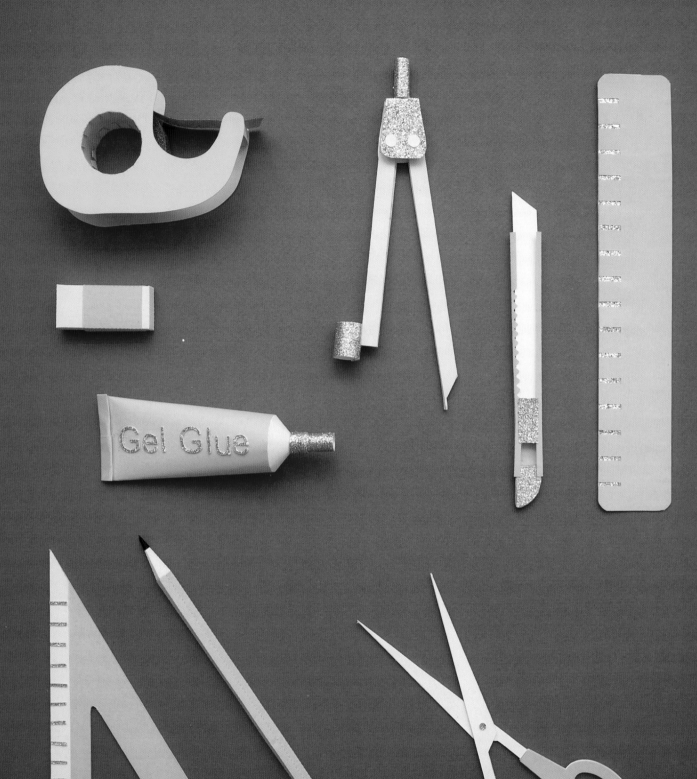

LAURE'S SECRETS

Behind the Scenes of a Creation

Basic Kit

Basic Techniques

Specific Techniques

BEHIND THE SCENES OF A CREATION

It takes me an average of three days to design a project, from the idea for it to taking photos of it. My surroundings, trends around me, and social networks are what mainly inspire me.

1
PLANNING AND DRAWING THE SHAPE

I always start by drawing the shape of the creation. Afterward, this base allows me to achieve the most-accurate volumes and form in the 3-D version.

2
PROTOTYPE ON WHITE PAPER

I draw and construct the creation with white paper. This paper does highlight flaws, but it's also more economical. This is the most complex stage because I make four prototypes on average before turning to color.

3 COLOR CHOICES

This step is the most difficult for me because the colors reveal the dimensions and bring out the magic. Sometimes I have to make the whole creation to realize that the colors don't work, and then I start all over again.

Gel Glue

4 ASSEMBLY OF THE ELEMENTS

My favorite stage! Everything comes together, and it's magic!

5 CLICK! CLICK!

Last step: taking photographs. This is a step that I especially work to get just right, because if the light or the shooting angle isn't good, the hours spent in making the paper object don't come across and are wasted.

BASIC KIT

TAPE

Useful for tracing a pattern. I prefer matte tape because it is easier to remove afterward.

INDISPENSABLES

An eraser and a pencil (a mechanical pencil keeps a sharp point). To avoid leaving an indent on the paper, don't press down too hard.

SCISSORS

Opt for pointed scissors, such as sewing scissors. Use them if you don't feel comfortable with a fixed-blade utility knife.

TRIANGLE

Also called a set square, this is perfect for drawing grids.

COMPASS

You might think that I use it mainly for tracing circles. You'd be wrong; it's the best way to make a small hole in the paper!

FIXED-BLADE UTILITY KNIFE (CUTTER)

I use this sort of craft knife for cutting and folding. I recommend using it to be more precise, because it forces us to concentrate and therefore work slower.

RULER

I use it for the majority of straight cuts I make with a cutter. Opt for a plastic ruler to avoid leaving marks on the paper.

GEL GLUE

You can make beautiful cuts and folds, but if you don't have the right glue, your project can quickly turn into a nightmare. Choose a brand with solvent that dries quickly and adheres!

PAPER

Textured or smooth? It doesn't matter . . . for me it's the color that counts. Smooth papers will generally have bright colors, unlike papers showing the grain, which often have softer colors. For more solid and longer-lasting work, I use paper between 160 and 200 gsm (grams per square meter). As a reference point, a sheet of standard copy or printer paper is around 80 gsm. The papers used for the creations in this book come from the Clairefontaine line (Maya and Etival collections), unless otherwise indicated.

BASIC TECHNIQUES

REPRODUCING A PATTERN

Each of the projects includes actual-size patterns (except for the cuckoo clock, p. 58, where the pattern is at 50% of actual size).

MATERIALS

Pattern

Colored paper

Tracing paper

Pencil

Eraser (if needed)

Scissors

LEGEND

——— cutting line

×   gluing area

●   where to make
a hole

1   Place the tracing paper onto the pattern.

2   Trace the outline with a pencil, as well as the cutting lines, the folding lines, the location of the hole, and the drawing. Don't trace the gluing areas. To make sure your reproduction is perfect, don't hesitate to use a ruler for straight lines.

3   Turn the tracing paper over and place it on the paper you are going to use.

4   Go over the traced lines with a pencil.

5   Cut out the pattern.

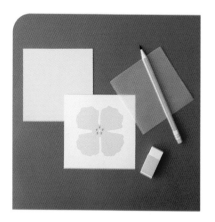

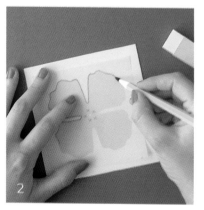

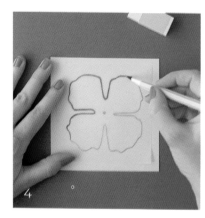
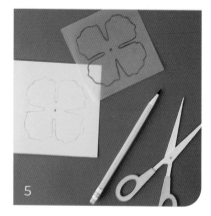

FOLDING

MATERIALS

Pattern
Colored paper
Tracing paper
Pencil
Eraser (if needed)
Scissors
Cutter
Ruler

KEY

————— cutting line

- - - - - folding line

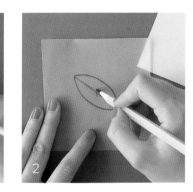

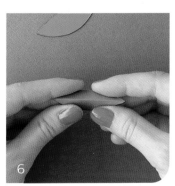

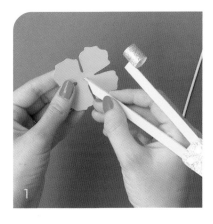

1   Place the tracing paper onto the pattern; trace the outline and the folding line with a pencil.

2   To separate the outline and the fold, make a mark on the folding line.

3   Turn the tracing paper over and place it on the paper you are going to use.

4   Cut out the outline first.

5   Using the ruler as a guide, draw the blunt side of the cutter along the folding line.

6   Fold the paper.

MAKING A HOLE

MATERIALS

Your cutout pattern
Compass
Toothpick or skewer

Key

● where to make the hole

1   Make a hole in the pattern where indicated, using the point of the compass.

2   Enlarge the hole with a toothpick or skewer according to the project instructions.

SHAPING THE PATTERN

MATERIALS

Cutout pattern

Ruler

Hold the pattern between your fingers and bend the desired places, using your ruler.

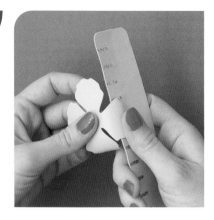

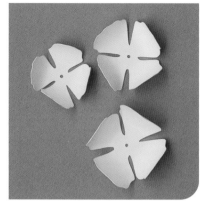

GLUING

MATERIALS

Cutout pattern
Glue

1. Paste the backside of the pattern by following the gluing areas indicated on the pattern.

2. Paste and overlay as indicated in the project instructions. Press lightly with your finger until the glue is dry.

Tip: For patterns with tabs, it's better to glue the part where the tab will be applied, so that your project remains as clean as possible.

BONUS: YOUR TURN

With these techniques, you can easily make an anemone on a stem.

1. Trace the petals of the anemone and the leaves found in "The Garden" chapter (pp. 138 and 140).

2. Mark the folds of the leaves.

3. Shape the petals.

4. Insert and glue the petals one by one onto a skewer.

5. Glue the leaves under the anemone.

SPECIFIC TECHNIQUES

LAYERING

This technique gives depth and nothing is easier to do!

See:
- Shellfish Board (p. 20)
- California Polaroid (p. 64)
- Lunar Decoration (p. 82)
- Llama Mobile (p. 90)
- Peacock Headboard (p. 108)
- Potted Plants (p. 118)

MATERIALS

Cutout pattern
Glue

Paste the pieces on top of each other as shown in the photos
(for the lemons, see p. 24).

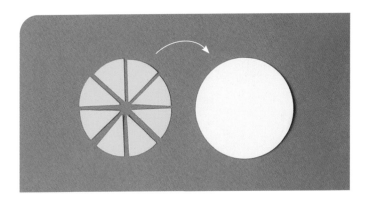

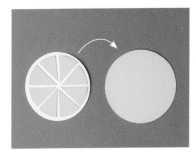

LAYERING WITH DEPTH

This technique isn't exactly 3-D, but it gives the illusion of depth.

See:
- Shellfish Board (p. 20)
- Teapot Aquarium (p. 38)
- Palm Lamp (p. 52)
- California Polaroid (p. 64)

MATERIALS

Cutout pattern

Strip of paper

Cutter or scissors

Glue

Ruler

1. As if it were curling ribbon, use the ruler or scissors to curl this previously cut strip to the desired dimensions.

2. Wrap the strip on itself and glue its end.

3. Stick it to the back of the piece.

This technique is flexible; you'll see that the rolled paper strip can be replaced by foam core, rice grains, or shells or placed between different layers of paper.

FOLD IN AND FOLD OUT

This is the fan technique, which easily adds dimension without gluing.

KEY

- - - - - - - fold line for folding out (mountain fold: MF)

— — line for folding in (valley fold: VF)

See:
- Palm Lamp (p. 52)
- California Polaroid (p. 64)
- Llama Mobile (p. 90)
- Parrot Mirror (p. 100)
- Potted Plants (p. 118)
- Flower Wreath (p. 134)

MATERIALS

Cutout pattern
Cutter
Scissors
Ruler

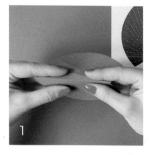
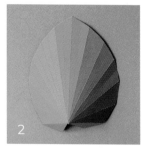

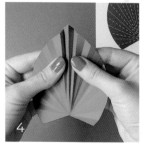
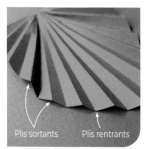

Plis sortants   Plis rentrants

1   Trace the pattern, copy it onto the paper, and cut it out. Mark the fold lines and use the ruler and the blunt edge of the cutter to indent them. To dissociate the MF from the VF, mark them while you are tracing the pattern.

2   Fold one mark out of two.

3   Flip the paper and fold the remaining marks.

4   Retighten the folds like a fan.

SEMI-VOLUME

Here is a quick and easy method to get dimension.
A snip of the scissors, a little glue, and you have volume!

See:

- Insects in a Bell Jar (p. 46)
- Cuckoo Clock (p. 58)
- Parrot Mirror (p. 100)
- Potted plants (p. 118)

MATERIALS

Cutout pattern
Scissors
Glue

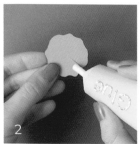

1   Cut into the shape following the cutting line.

2   Add a little glue to the left side of the slit.

3   Overlay and glue the right side of the slit to the left. To get a more pronounced dimension, cut a larger slit.

ROUNDED VOLUME

This technique requires finesse in cutting and gluing.

See:
- Hanging Vegetables (p. 28)
- Aquarium Teapot (p. 38)
- Whale Piggy Bank (p. 76)
- Lunar Decoration (p. 82)

MATERIALS

Cutout pattern

Glue

1 Mark the folds.

2 Turn the piece over and glue the part closest to the intermediate tab.

3 Glue the tab.

4 Repeat this for all tabs in the same row.

5 Do the same for the top row.

6 Glue the outer tabs that will be used to gather the two sides of the piece.

7 Glue.

8 Close the rest of the piece.

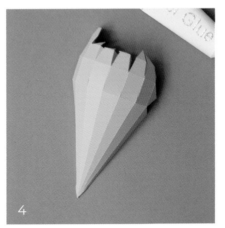
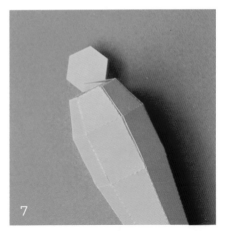
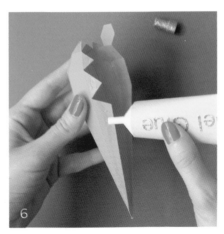

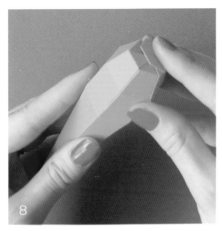

Liste de
COURSES

Boucherie   Épicerie

Poissonnerie   Gourmandise

Fruits et légumes   Boisson

Boulangerie   Hygiène

Laitage   Entretien

Surgelé   Autre

THE KITCHEN

Shellfish Board

Hanging Vegetables

Teapot Aquarium

SHELLFISH BOARD

As simple and quick as preparing a plate of shellfish,
this chopping board will easily find its place in your kitchen!

MATERIALS

* Basic kit (see pp. 10–11)

* 6 sheets (letter size):

  - Red × 1
  - Orange × 1
  - Blue × 1
  - Antique green × 1
  - Mint green × 1
  - Yellow × 1
  - White × 1

* Baking paper or tracing paper

* Wooden board

* Black felt-tip pen

* White felt-tip pen (optional)

PAPER

Red shrimp
🔴 Red

Orange shrimp
🟠 Orange

Body of the crab
🔴 Red

Shell of the crab
⚫ Midnight blue

Parsley
🟢 Antique green

Lime
🟢 Antique green   🟢 Mint green   ⚪ White

Lemon
🟡 Lemon yellow   ⚪ White

Leek
🟢 Antique green   🟢 Mint green

PATTERN KEY

O   eyes drawn with black felt-tip pen

×   gluing area

——   cutting line

DIMENSIONS

Wooden board (chopping surface):
$5^{15}\!/_{16} \times 11^{13}\!/_{16}$ in. (15 × 30 cm)

THE SHRIMP

1   Trace the pattern of the shrimp and transfer it to the red paper (see "Basic Techniques: Reproducing a Pattern," p. 12).

2   With the scissors, cut the outlines and cutting lines of the tail and head.

3   Use the ruler to shape the head and tail of the shrimp (see "Shaping the Pattern," p. 14).

4   To form the abdomen, cut a $\frac{9}{16}$ × $11\frac{13}{16}$ in. (1.5 × 30 cm) strip out of the red paper.

5   Curl this strip with scissors.

6   Stick the end of the strip onto the body of the shrimp (before the start of the tail), wrap the strip around the rest of the body, and then stick the end of the strip opposite the tail.

7   Glue the head to the upper abdomen, as shown in the photograph. Draw the eyes with the black felt-tip pen, using the markers on the gauge.

8   To make the shrimp antennae, cut two thin strips of red paper. Curl them with your ruler before sticking them under the head of the shrimp.

9   Repeat these steps to make the orange shrimp.

TO MAKE IT MORE REALISTIC

You can double the band of the abdomen: one red and one orange.

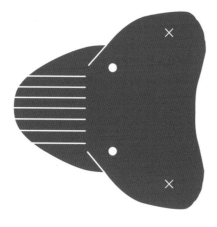

Shrimp head

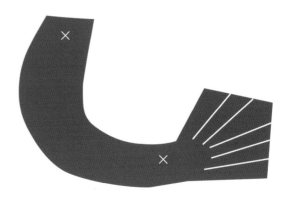

Shrimp tail

THE CRAB

1. As with the shrimp, trace the patterns and transfer them to the paper (red for the body and blue for the shell).

2. With a black felt-tip pen, trace the pincers and eyes.

3. Use the ruler to shape the middle of the shell and the legs of the crab.

4. Run a little glue at the high and low ends of the shell and bend it slightly before inserting the body.

5. Press to glue the shell on both sides of the body.

Crab head

Crab shell

THE LEMONS

1 Separately trace the circle of the outer edge of the lemon, as well as the smallest circle with the quarters. Transfer them to the yellow paper.

2 Trace the outline of the white circle. Transfer it to the white paper.

3 Cut all the circles, then cut eight quarters out of the smallest circle, following the markers indicated on the pattern.

4 Glue the white circle onto the larger one, then glue the quarters slightly spaced (see "Specific Techniques: Layering," p. 15).

5 Repeat these steps for the second yellow lemon and the lime.

TO MAKE IT MORE REALISTIC

You can draw white drops on the different quarters, using a white felt-tip pen for example. To give dimension, use different shades for the outline and wedges of the lemons.

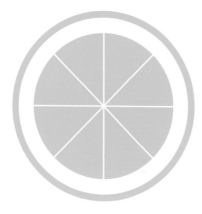

Lemon

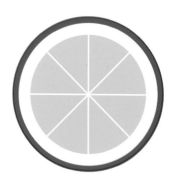

Lime

PARSLEY

1 Trace the pattern of the parsley leaf and transfer it six times onto the green paper, then cut them out. You can make as many leaves as you like.

2 Give dimension to the leaves with your thumbnail.

Parsley

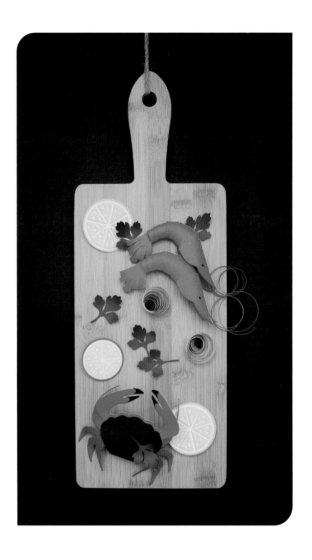

THE LEEK SLICES

1 Cut a ⅜ × 11¹³⁄₁₆ in. (1 x 30 cm) strip from baking paper (or tracing paper), then two others of the same size from green papers.

2 Curl these strips with the scissors.

3 Glue the three strips end to end in this order: tracing paper, mint-green paper, then antique-green paper. Wrap to form a circle and stick the end.

4 Repeat these steps to make another slice.

MOUNTING

Glue the different elements to the board, as shown in the photo. To give more dimension to the lemons, you can affix them on shells or rice grains.

HANGING VEGETABLES

Nothing could be simpler to make a good soup than carrots, leeks, radishes, and, above all, a pinch of patience. But first, go to the market to find the ingredients.

MATERIALS

* Basic kit (see pp. 10–11)

* 9 sheets (letter size):

  - Dark pink × 1
  - Fuchsia × 1
  - Orange × 1
  - White × 1
  - Brown × 1
  - Mint green × 1
  - Spruce green × 1
  - Antique green × 2

* Decorative grid

* Basket and wooden board (optional)

* String

PAPER (185gsm, unless otherwise indicated)

Radish leaves
● Antique green

Top of the radish
● Fuchsia (160 gsm)

Point of the radish
● Dark pink (160 gsm)

Carrot tops
● Antique green   ● Pine green

Carrot
● Orange (160 gsm)

Leek leaves
● Antique green   ● Mint green

White of the leek
○ White

Radish and leek roots
● Brown

PATTERN KEY

———— cutting line

········ folding line

×   gluing area

+   area where the radish and leek roots are inserted

DIMENSIONS

Decorative grid: 17¾ × 23⅝ in. (45 × 60 cm)

Wooden board (chopping surface):
6⁵⁄₁₆ × 9¹⁄₁₆ in. (16 × 23 cm)

RADISH LEAVES

1　Trace the pattern of the leaves. Transfer them to the antique-green paper, then cut them out (see "Basic Techniques: Reproducing a Pattern," p. 12).

2　Tape the thin ends of the leaves together.

3　Fold just above the tape.

4　Shape the leaves with the ruler (see "Basic Techniques: Shaping the Pattern," p. 14) and set aside.

RADISH TIP

1　Trace the pattern of the radish tip. Transfer it to the dark-pink paper and cut it out.

2　Run the back of your blade along the dotted lines to mark the folds (see "Basic Techniques: Folding," p. 13).

3　To form the roots of the radish, cut three thin strips 1⁄16 in. (2 mm) wide and 2 in. (5 cm) long out of the brown paper, then attach them together by one end with tape.

4　Place these roots at the top of the radish tip, as shown in the pattern, then close the piece by gluing the tab to the nearest part. The tape blocks the roots.

5　Put this piece aside.

Pattern (*right*): radish leaves

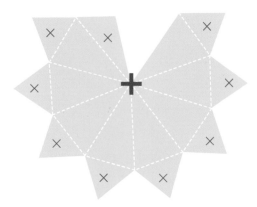

Pattern (*center*): radish tip

RADISH

1　Trace the pattern of the top of the radish. Transfer it to the fuschia paper, then cut it out, without forgetting the slot in the middle of the octagon.

2　Run the back of your blade along the dotted lines. Gently erase the lines and then mark the folds.

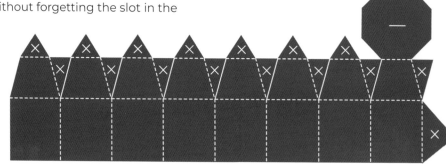

Pattern (*bottom*): radish

ASSEMBLING THE RADISH

1   Glue each remaining tab of the tip of the radish on the straight side of the top radish strip, then glue the two top radish tabs to the other end to close the strip.

2   Shape the top of the radish by gluing the intermediate tabs on the nearest parts (see "Specific Techniques: Rounded Volume," p. 17).

3   Insert the radish leaves into the slot of the octagon and stick them if necessary.

4   Close the radish by sticking the octagon on the triangular tabs.

5   Repeat these steps until you have the desired number of radishes.

THE CARROT TOPS

1 Trace the pattern of the carrot tops.

2 Transfer them to the green paper and then cut them out. Run the back of your blade along the dotted lines. Gently erase the lines and then mark the folds.

TO MAKE THEM MORE REALISTIC

You can use two different shades of green paper.

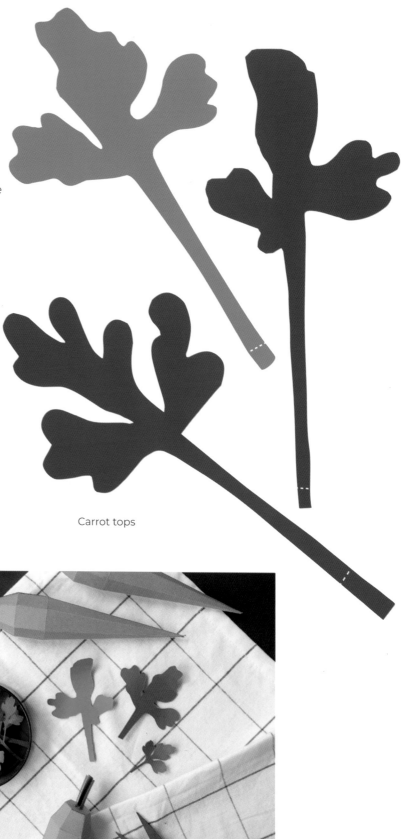

Carrot tops

1   Trace the pattern of the carrot. Transfer it to the orange paper, then cut it out. Don't forget the slots in the hexagon.

2   Run the back of your blade lightly along the dotted lines. Gently erase the lines and then mark the folds.

3   Turn the paper so that the tip forms a cone.

4   Glue the intermediate tabs on the nearest parts, starting with the A band and then the B band. Close the piece by gluing the tabs on the C side to the nearest end.

5   Insert the tops into the slots and glue them if necessary.

6   Close the core by gluing the hexagon onto the triangular tabs.

7   Repeat these steps until you have the desired number of carrots.

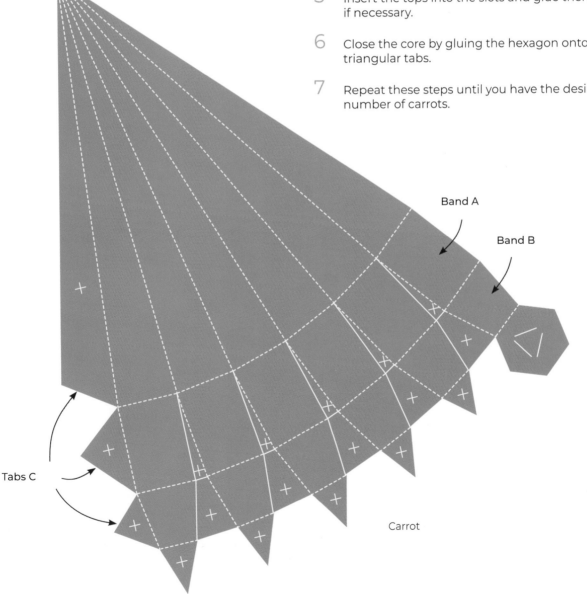

Band A

Band B

Tabs C

Carrot

LEEKS

LEEK WHITE

1   Trace the pattern of the leek white. Transfer it to the white paper, then cut it out. Don't forget the slot on the octagon.

2   Run the back of your blade lightly along the dotted lines. Gently erase the lines and then mark the folds.

3   Turn the paper to form a cylinder. Glue the intermediate tabs on the nearest parts.

4   Close the cylinder by gluing the tabs on the big side to the nearest part.

5   To form the roots of the leek, cut eight thin strips ⅟₁₆ in. (2 mm) wide and 2 in. (5 cm) long out of the brown paper, then fasten them together by one end with tape.

6   Insert the roots into the slot of the octagon and glue them if necessary.

7   Close the leek by sticking the hexagon on the triangular tabs.

8   Finally, give shape to the cutout parts at the other end.

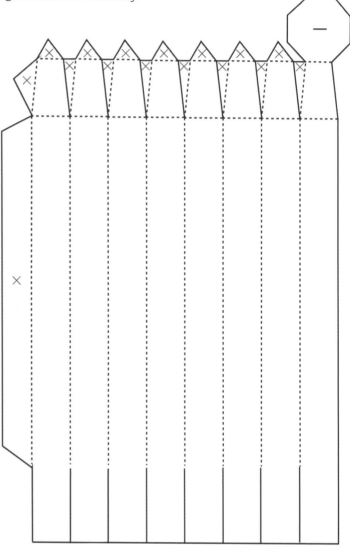

Leek white

LEEK LEAVES

1 Trace the pattern of the leek leaf. Transfer it four times to the dark-green paper and twice to the light-green paper and then cut it out.

2 Trace, transfer, and then cut the support out of the dark-green paper.

3 Run the back of your blade lightly along the dotted lines. Gently erase the lines and then mark the folds.

4 Place a dark-green strip in another of the same color; glue it to the tip of the support (see the diagram). In the same way, glue two other dark-green leaves under them. Do the same for both light-green leaves.

5 Paste the two strips and then insert the leaves into the leek white.

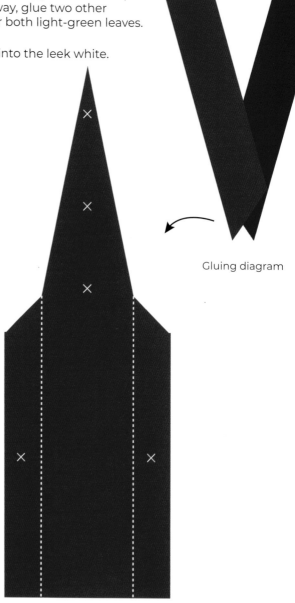

Gluing diagram

Leek leaf
(2 x mint green and 4 x antique green)

Leaf support

SETTING UP

Hang these vegetables by tying them to a decorative grid, or by making a hole with a compass at the end of the leaves to pass the string through. These vegetables would also look good in a basket.

TEAPOT AQUARIUM

Before you can relax in your kitchen and watch it, this fish will require meticulous gluing of its surrounding plants and precision in cutting it out.

MATERIALS

* Basic kit (see pp. 10–11)

* 5 sheets (letter size):
  - Pink × 1
  - Fuchsia × 1
  - Orange × 1
  - White × 1
  - Red × 1

* Tracing paper

* ³⁄₁₆ in. (0.5 cm) thick foam core

* Transparent teapot

* Paper punch

* Fishing line

* Skewer

* Black felt-tip pen

* Yellow felt-tip pen

* White felt-tip pen (optional)

PAPER (185 g)

Fish
● Red

Plants, layers 3 and 6
● Pink

Plants, layers 2 and 5
● Fuchsia

Plants, layer 1
● Orange

Fish and plants, layer 4
● Tracing paper

Fish's eyes
○ White

PATTERN KEY

——— cutting line

········ folding line

✕ gluing area

DIMENSIONS

Teapot: H 5¹⁵⁄₁₆ in. × W 2¹⁵⁄₁₆ in. (H 15 cm x W 7.5 cm)

(nothing is glued to the teapot)

THE SEABED

1. Trace the patterns of the plants as well as those of the seabed layers. For plants in layers 5 and 6, reproduce them once on pink paper and once on fuchsia paper (see "Basic Techniques: Reproduce a Pattern," p. 12).
Tip: Adjust the length of the layers to the size of your teapot.

2. Glue the plants on each layer of the same color, referring to the pattern keys and the gluing areas.

3. Draw six ⅜ × 2¾ in. (1 × 7 cm) strips onto the foam core and cut them out with a cutter.
Tip: Adjust the length of these strips to the size of your teapot.

4. Cut six ⅜ × 2¾ in. (1 × 7 cm) strips (two pink, two fuchsia, one orange, and one white). Glue them on top of the foam core strips.

5. Glue the layers to the back of the strips of the same color.

SETTING THEM INTO THE TEAPOT

1. Insert the layers one by one in the teapot, positioning them as shown in the photos (see pp. 38 and 41). You can fold the plants so that they fit more easily through the top of the teapot.

To make them more stable:

You can stick a few layers together before placing them in the teapot.

1. Using a skewer, slide the front layers and the right and left layers on either side of the seabed (they are kept in place by the sides of the teapot).

THE FISH

THE DORSAL FIN

1. Trace the patterns of the dorsal fin (see p. 42). Transfer them to the red paper and the tracing paper and cut them out.

2. Cut 7⅞ in. (20 cm) of fishing line, then tape one of its ends to one of the red elements so that the line protrudes upward.

3. Glue these red elements on each side of the paper layer by aligning the tips. Remember to hide the tape that holds the line.

Layer 6: pink

Layer 5: fuchsia

Layer 4: tracing paper

Layer 3: pink

Layer 2: fuchsia

Layer 1: orange

Front layer: pink

Right layer: pink

Left layer: pink

Plant layer 1: orange

Plant layer 2: fuchsia

Plant layers 5 + 6:
(1 x pink, 1 x fuchsia)

Plant layer 4: tracing paper

Plant layer 3: pink

THE VENTRAL FINS

4 Trace the patterns of the ventral fins. Transfer them to the corresponding papers, then cut them out.

Tip: The pencil may not show up clearly, so feel free to press hard to mark the paper.

5 Paste the red parts to the tracing paper, aligning the tips.

THE TAIL

6 Trace the patterns of the tail. Transfer them to the corresponding papers and cut them out.

7 Glue a red element onto each tracing paper element.

THE EYES

8 Using a paper punch, cut two circles out of the white paper.

9 Color these two circles with the yellow felt-tip pen.

10 Draw and then color a circle with the black felt-tip pen.

FOR MORE REALISM

You can add a small white dot to the black circle, using a white felt-tip.

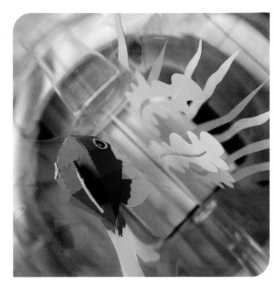

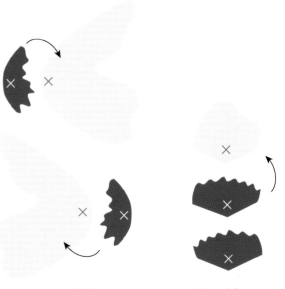

Fish eye

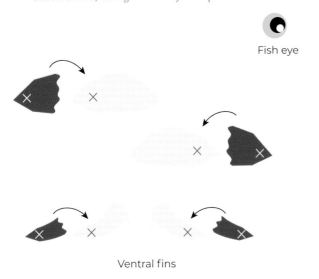

Ventral fins

Tail

Dorsal fin

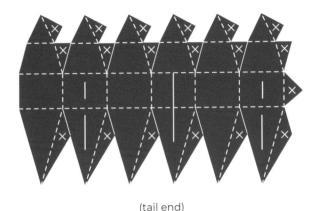

Fish body
(head end)

(tail end)

THE BODY

11 Trace the pattern of the body. Transfer it to the red paper and cut it out, without forgetting the slits indicated on the pattern.

12 Run the back of your blade along the dotted lines. Gently erase the lines and mark the folds.

13 Glue each intermediate tab on the head side to the nearest part. Continue with the tabs of the head, then those on the tail side (see "Specific Techniques: Rounded Volume," p. 17).

14 Close the body piece by gluing the end tabs to the nearest parts.

ASSEMBLY

15 Insert the dorsal fin into the largest slot.

16 Insert the small ventral fins into the two small slots, then the other two into the remaining slots.

17 Glue the two tails face to face at the end of the body of the fish.

18 Finish by gluing the eyes.

INSTALLATION IN THE TEAPOT

19 Place the fish in the teapot and close the lid to secure the fishing line outside.

20 Wrap the rest of the line around the lid and tie a knot. Cut the excess line.

THE LIVING ROOM

Insects in a Bell Jar

Palm Lamp

Cuckoo Clock

California Polaroid

INSECTS IN A BELL JAR

Making insects out of paper is easier than catching real ones!

MATERIALS

* Basic kit (see page pp. 10–11)

* 4 metallic papers (letter size):

    - Gold × 2
    - Blue × 1
    - Pink × 1

* 5¹⁵⁄₁₆ × 5¹⁵⁄₁₆ in. (15 × 15 cm) foam core 1 cm thick

* Glass bell with base

* 3 skewers

PAPER (185 gsm)

Golden insect
Gold metallic paper

Blue insect
Blue metallic paper

Pink insect
Pink metallic paper

PATTERN KEY

———— cutting line

·········· folding line (outward angle)

— — — folding line (inward angle)

×   gluing area

○   hole

DIMENSIONS

Bell jar: 5¹⁵⁄₁₆ × 11 in. (15 x 28 cm)

THE GOLDEN SCARAB

1   Trace the patterns of the beetle (see "Basic Techniques: Reproducing a Pattern," p. 12). Transfer them to the metallic paper and cut them out.

Tip: The pencil may not show up clearly, so feel free to press down to mark the paper.

2   Run the back of your blade along the folding lines. Mark the folds (see "Basic Techniques: Folding," p. 13).

3   With the compass, make a hole in the legs, as shown. Insert a skewer to widen the hole, then remove it (see "Basic Techniques: Making a Hole," p. 13).

4   Slide and glue the corners of the body of the bug where indicated (see "Specific Techniques: Half Volume," p. 16).

5   As with the body, slide and glue the corners of the bug's shell to the indicated areas.

6   Slide and glue the elements of the head of the bug, as shown on the pattern.

7   Stick the tabs of the body on the central part of the bug's legs.

8   Glue the head tab to the body (big legs), ensuring to align the points folded previously. Finish by sticking the shell to the body of the beetle.

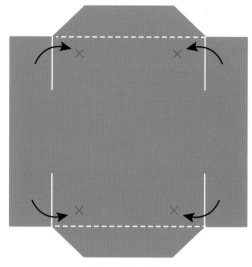

Scarab body

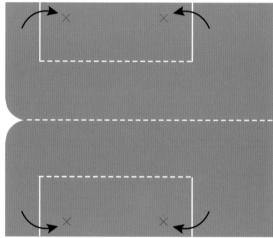

Scarab shell

1 cm
0,5 cm
1 cm

Diagram, pinking the base

Scarab legs

Scarab head

Insect legs

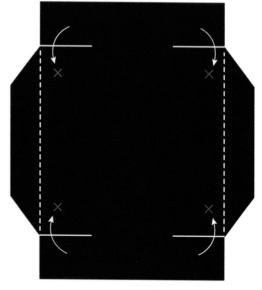

Insect body

THE BLUE AND PINK INSECTS

1   Trace the patterns of the insect. Transfer them to the blue and pink metallic papers, then cut them out.

2   Run the back of your blade on the folding lines. Erase the lines and mark the folds.

3   With the compass, make a hole in the legs, as shown. Insert a skewer to widen the holes and remove it.

4   Slide and glue the body corners to specified locations.

5   As with the body, slide and glue the corners of the shells where indicated.

6   Glue the body tabs on the central part of the insect legs.

7   Fold the center of the shells so that the edges are inward.

8   Glue the shells onto the bodies, bringing out the front that symbolizes the head.

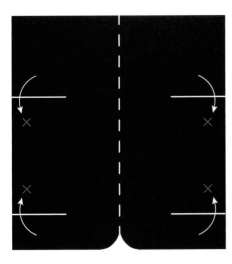

Insect shell

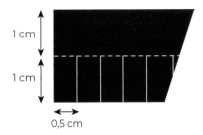

1 cm

1 cm

0,5 cm

Diagram, pinking the base

1   Draw a circle a little smaller than the width of the bell jar on the gold metallic paper, then cut it out (here, the circle is 5⅛ in. [13 cm] in diameter).

2   Transfer this circle to the foam core, then cut it out with a cutter.

3   Calculate the perimeter of the circle with the mathematical formula $2\pi r$ and add ⅜ in. (1 cm) (for example, here: 2 × 3.14 × 2⁹⁄₁₆ in. [6.5 cm] + ⅜ in. [1 cm] = 16⁷⁄₁₆ in. [41.82 cm]).

4   From the metallic paper, draw a strip ¹³⁄₁₆ in. (2 cm) wide and of the previously defined length and cut it out. Then draw a line connecting the center of the small sides. Run the back of your blade along the dotted lines and mark the fold.

Tip: If your sheet is smaller than the length found, make two strips and assemble them end to end.

5   Pink with the scissors, as shown in the diagram.

6   Glue the notches to the top of the foam core circle.

7   Glue the gold circle over the notches and the foam core.

8   With the compass, make three holes in a triangle (here, the triangle measures 2 in. [5 cm] on the side).

9   Insert the skewers under the legs of the insects, then pin them to the base.

Tip: Tilt the insects to fit them under the bell.

INSTALLATION

Place the base with the insects onto the base of the bell jar and enclose them them under the glass.

PALM LAMP

Add the glamour of the palm tree motif to a lamp.
It's easy, as long as you like paper cutting.

MATERIALS

Basic kit (see pp. 10–11)

7 sheets (letter size):

- Gold × 7

 Gold lamp base

Rotary cutter (optional)

Glue gun

Decorative bulb (50 W maximum)

Gold spray paint

PAPER

Palm tree
- Frosted gold, 150 gsm (my example uses Daler-Rowney Canford paper)

PATTERN KEY

——— cutting line

·········· folding line

×   gluing area

DIMENSIONS

Lamp base: H 13¾ in. (35 cm) × L 5½ in. (14 cm)

PREPARING THE LAMP'S BASE

1. If the socket on your base isn't gold, mask off the part near the socket with tape.

2. Shake the spray paint can, then spray the outside of the socket.
   Tip: Use the spray outdoors and on a protective cardboard.

3. Spray the ring that is screwed onto the socket.

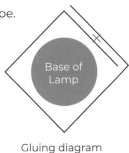

Gluing diagram

PALM TREE'S TRUNK

1. Trace the bark 1 pattern (see "Basic Techniques: Reproducing a Pattern," on p. 12). Transfer it eighteen times to the gold paper and cut out the outlines.
   Tip: Start by transferring the bark pattern to the corner of your sheet, then place the following ones as close together as you can to make the most of the surface area.

2. Use the reverse side of your blade to make a slight indent on the folding lines. Erase the lines and mark the folds (see "Basic Techniques: Folding," on p. 13).

3. Glue one of the petal areas at the end of the bark, then wrap the bark around the lamp base and glue two petals together (see gluing diagram). Repeat this fifteen more times.

4. Mount a bark piece under the lamp socket. Spray a dot of glue on the bottom of each petal, then add a second bark piece by rotating it 45° in relation to the first (refer to the gluing areas indicated on the patterns and in the diagram).

   Repeat this fifteen more times.
   Tip: Once the glue has been applied, quickly interlock the pieces of bark because the glue hardens quickly.

If the lamp cord is ¹³⁄₁₆ in. (2 cm) from the base:

5. Trace the bark patterns 2 and 3. Transfer them to the gold paper and cut out the outlines.

6. Use the reverse side of your blade to make a slight indent on the folding lines. Erase the lines and mark the folds.

7. Glue bark 2 in the same way as bark 1 by wrapping it around the base of the lamp.

8. Repeat this for bark 3. It is not necessary to glue the edges because these two barks touch the base of the lamp.

If the cord is in the base:

9. Add two bark 1 pieces under the others.

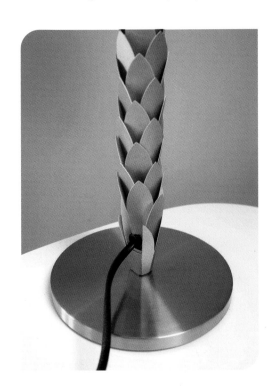

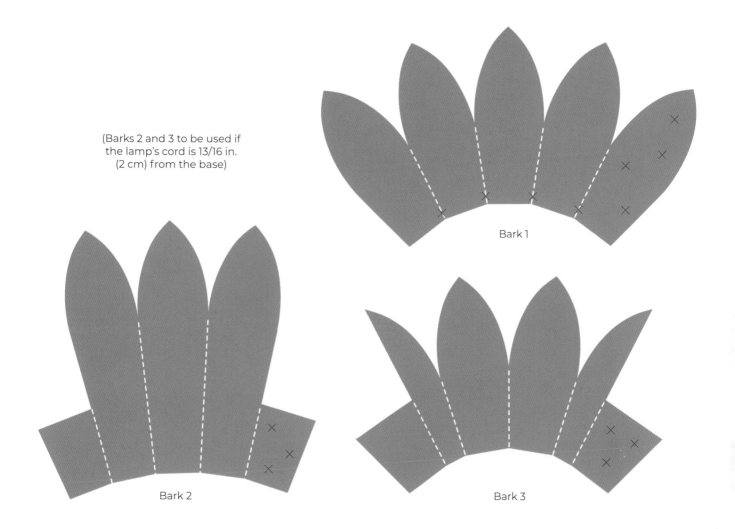

(Barks 2 and 3 to be used if the lamp's cord is 13/16 in. (2 cm) from the base)

Bark 1

Bark 2

Bark 3

PALM LEAVES

1   Trace the patterns of the three leaves (see p. 56). Transfer the large and medium leaves ten times to the gold paper and transfer the small one five times. Cut out the outlines.

2   Cut out the circles with a rotary cutter.

    Tip: If you don't have a rotary cutter, a plain cutter will do.

3   Place five large leaves in a star shape, then glue them together at the level of the circle. Repeat this to have two stars of large leaves, two stars of medium leaves, and one star of small leaves.

4   With the ruler, shape each sheet (see "Basic Techniques: Shaping the Pattern," p. 14).

5   Cut three strips of gold paper 3/16 in. (0.5 cm) wide and 5⅛ in. (13 cm) long. Curl them with scissors and glue the ends of each strip together to form three paper circles (see "Specific Techniques: Layering with Depth," p. 15) that will slip between each star of leaves (see steps 6 to 8).

6   Place a star of medium leaves onto the socket and insert the first circle of paper.

7   Place a star of large leaves onto the socket and insert the second circle of paper.

8 Place a star of large leaves back onto the socket and insert the third circle of paper.

9 Place a star of medium leaves onto the socket.

10 Insert the last star of small leaves on the screw ring.

11 Screw the ring onto the socket and then add the bulb.

Check that the diameters of the socket and screw ring are 1⅛ in. (2.8 cm) and 1¼ in. (3.2 cm). If the dimensions are different, change the size of the circles in the leaf patterns.

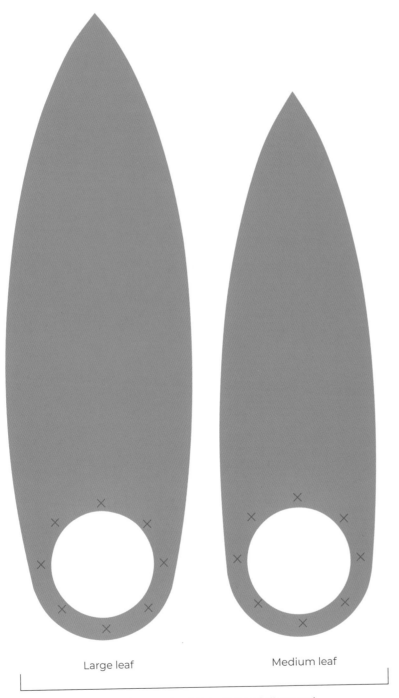

Large leaf

Medium leaf

Small leaf

(circle for a socket 1 ⅛ in. [2.8 cm] diameter)

(circle for a screw ring 1 ¼ in. [3.2 cm] diameter)

CUCKOO CLOCK

Inspired by Swiss cuckoo clocks, this standing or hanging clock is home to a small, silent bird. Cutting, gluing, and assembling are simple.

MATERIALS

* Basic kit (see pp. 10–11)

* 8 sheets (letter size):

    - Fuchsia × 4
    - Pink × 1
    - Blue × 1
    - Gold or yellow × 1
    - Ivory × 1

* Hands and clock mechanism

* Protractor (to make the corners of the right and left roofs)

* Paper punch

* Black felt-tip pen

* Nail (optional)

PAPER (185 gsm unless otherwise indicated)

Cuckoo
● Fuchsia (160 gsm)

Bird
● Light pink   ○ Ivory (160 gsm)
● Frosted gold (150 gsm) (my example uses Daler-Rowney Canford paper)

Flowers
● Fuchsia   ● Midnight blue

Cuckoo

PATTERN SCALE 1/2

PATTERN KEY

———— cutting line

-------- folding line

✕ gluing area

○ hole

DIMENSIONS

Cuckoo clock: width 7½ in. (19 cm) × height 9¹⁄₁₆ in. (23 cm) × depth 2⅜ in. (6 cm)

Clock hands: 2³⁄₁₆ in. (5.5 cm), 1⅜ in. (3.5 cm) and 1 in. (2.5 cm)

Mechanism: 2³⁄₁₆ × 2³⁄₁₆ in. (5.5 × 5.5 cm)

Central barrel length: ¼ in. (7 mm)

THE CLOCK

1 Enlarge the patterns of the cuckoo clock to scale 1, transfer them to fuchsia paper, and cut them out. Make sure to transfer the pattern of the clock's side twice.
Tip: Make strips at least ³⁄₈ in. (I cm) wide.

2 Make the hole that will accommodate the mechanism, starting with the tip of your compass, then insert a pencil until you get the desired width (see "Basic Techniques: Making a Hole," p. 13).

3 For the back of the clock, transfer the pattern of the front of the clock a second time (without the two circles). Draw a 2¾ × 2¾ in. (7 × 7 cm) square at ¹³⁄₁₆ in. (2 cm) from the bottom of the cuckoo clock and cut it out.

4 Run the back of your blade along the folding lines. Erase the lines and then mark the folds.

5 Glue the "clock's sides" on each side of the "bottom of the clock."

6 Close the bottom of the piece by gluing this large strip on tabs A, B, and C from the front and back of the clock.

7 Glue the triangular tab of the roof left D on the top of the right roof.

8 Glue the small tabs together to form the eaves of the roof.

9 Glue the roof to the tabs E and F on the front of the clock.

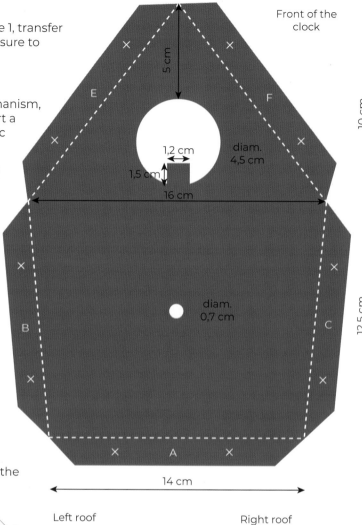

Front of the clock

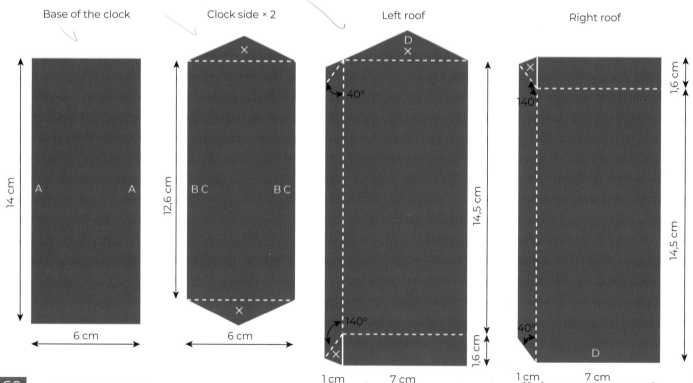

Base of the clock

Clock side × 2

Left roof

Right roof

THE BIRD

1   Trace the bird's patterns (see "Basic Techniques: Reproducing a Pattern," p. 12). Transfer them to the corresponding papers and cut them out. Don't forget the slit in the belly.

2   Run the back of the blade along the folding lines. Erase the lines and then mark the folds (see "Basic Techniques: Folding," p. 13).

3   Place the bird parts as shown in the pattern.

4   Glue the dark-pink bodies to the tops of the light-pink bodies.

5   Glue the back tab to the small end of the belly.

6   First stick the belly on the light-pink tabs, then the back on the dark-pink tabs.

7   In ivory paper, punch two small circles, draw the eyes with a black felt-tip pen, and stick them onto the bird.

8   Glue the beak to the bird, as shown in the pattern.

9   Glue the remaining tabs, as shown in the photo.

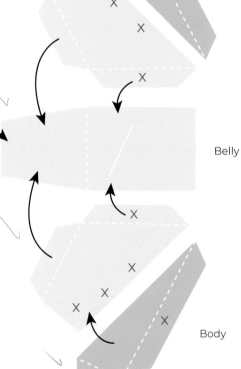

Body

Belly

Body

Back

Beak

LARGE FLOWER

Large petal
× 14

Large pistil
× 4

SMALL FLOWER

Small petal
× 28

Small pistil
× 4

1 Trace the flower patterns. Transfer them fourteen times for the large petals and twice for the large pistils, then twenty-eight times for the small petals and four times for the small pistils. Cut out all the elements in the corresponding papers.

Tip: To go faster, cut squares the size of the petals. Overlay several, transfer the petals to the top of the stacks, and cut them out.

2 Overlap and glue the right and left petal tabs to the central tab (see "Specific Techniques: Half Volume," p. 16).

FOR MORE REALISM

Vary the incline of the petal angle by moving the right tab more or less closer to the left.

3 Glue three petals at their base by placing them in staggered rows. Glue the other four petals outside the previous three.

4 Repeat the operation with the other petals.

5 Run the back of the blade along the folding lines of the pistils.

6 With the scissors, make notches in the folding lines to form a sun and then mark the folds.

7 Glue each pistil to the center of the flowers.

ASSEMBLY

1 Place the mechanism into the hole you made for it and insert the hands.

2 Glue all flowers as shown in the photo (see p. 61).

3 Insert the tab of the opening circle into the belly of the bird.

INSTALLATION

Hammer the nail into the wall and place the clock's hanging hole on the nail. You can also simply display the clock on a piece of furniture.

CALIFORNIA POLAROID

As with a real picture taken with a Polaroid, you'll need patience and a small dose of concentration for the image to be revealed.

MATERIALS

* Basic kit (see pp. 10–11)
* 14 sheets (letter size):
    - White × 4
    - Ivory × 1
    - Antique green × 1
    - Khaki green × 1
    - Royal blue × 1
    - Midnight blue × 1
    - Yellow × 1
    - Dark pink × 1
    - Light pink × 1
    - Fuchsia × 1
    - Gray × 1
* Photo frame
* Glue gun
* Nail (optional)
* 1 skewer
* 6 toothpicks

PAPER (185 gsm unless otherwise indicated)

Polaroid
○ White (270 g)

Plants
● Antique green   ● Khaki green

Ground
○ White   ○ Light pink

Towel
○ White   ● Dark pink

Swimming pool
○ White   ● Midnight blue   ● Royal blue
● Yellow   ● Light gray

Umbrellas
● Fuchsia (160 g)

PATTERN
SCALE
1

PATTERN KEY

——— cutting line

········ folding line (outward angle)

– – – folding line (inward angle)

✕ gluing area

○ hole

DIMENSIONS

Photo frame: 7½ × 9¹³⁄₁₆ in. (19 × 25 cm)
(Polaroid camera created by Laure)

1   Draw the face and bottom of the Polaroid frame by transferring the dimensions to white paper, then cut it out (see "Basic Techniques: Reproducing a Pattern," p. 12).

2   With the tip of your compass, make a hole in the bottom of the Polaroid at the point indicated on the pattern. Enlarge it with a skewer (see "Basic Techniques: Making a Hole," p. 13).

3   Trace the pattern of the inner frame of the Polaroid (see p. 68). Transfer the outlines and folding lines to four copies of white paper and cut them out.

4   Place the transferred pattern on one of the strips, transfer the pink line, then cut with a cutter. Do the same for the blue and green lines on two other strips.

Note: These colored lines are the markers that will tell you where to insert the plants on the different strips (see explanations on p. 72).

5   Run the blunt edge of the blade along the folding lines. Erase the lines and mark the folds. Fold the large tabs in one direction and the small ones in another.

6   Place the blue line strip, the green line strip, and the pink line strip together so that the previously cut lines are as close as possible to you.

7   Glue each small tab to the adjacent strip. To form a square, join the last two strips, making sure that the tabs are outside the square. If necessary, refer to the diagram (see p. 68).

8   Glue the large tabs to the edge of the inner square from the face of the Polaroid.

9   Draw the outer strips (length and width) twice, transferring the dimensions onto white paper, then cut them out.

10   Run the blunt edge of the blade along the folding lines. Erase the lines and mark the folds in the same direction (see "Basic Techniques: Folding," p. 13).

11   Glue the strips together alternately: a small, a large, a small, a large until you obtain a rectangle. This time, the tabs must be placed inside the rectangle (see the diagram on p. 68).

12   Glue the large tabs of this rectangle to the outline of the Polaroid face.

14   Glue the bottom to the remaining large tabs.

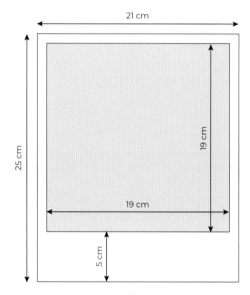

Front of Polaroid

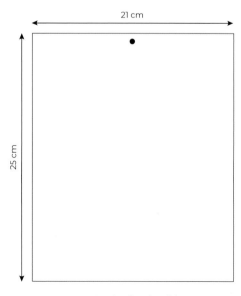

Back of Polaroid

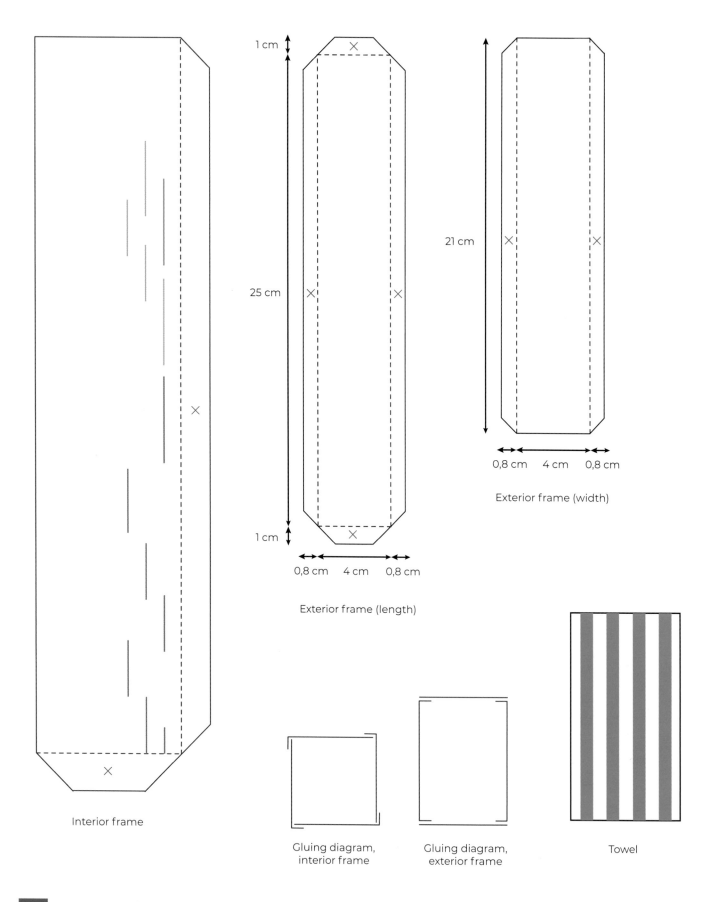

Interior frame

1 cm

25 cm

1 cm

0,8 cm   4 cm   0,8 cm

Exterior frame (length)

21 cm

0,8 cm   4 cm   0,8 cm

Exterior frame (width)

Gluing diagram,
interior frame

Gluing diagram,
exterior frame

Towel

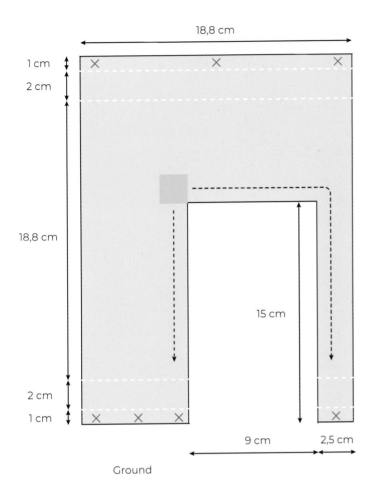

Ground

THE GROUND

1 Draw the ground by transferring the external dimensions to the ivory paper, then cut it out.

2 Run the blunt edge of the blade along the folding lines. Erase the lines and mark the folds. Reserve.

3 Draw a grid on half a pink leaf, spacing the lines by $^{13}/_{16}$ in. (2 cm).

4 First cut the strips, stack them, and cut about sixty squares.

5 Glue the first square as shown on the pattern, then glue the ones around the pool by spacing them $^1/_8$ or $^3/_{16}$ in. (3 or 4 mm) apart. Finish by aligning all the other squares with the previous ones to fill in the entirety of the ground surface.

6 Cut off the excess paper from the squares of the outer edge if necessary.

THE TOWELS

1 Draw three rectangles of $1^3/_{16}$ × $2^3/_{16}$ (3 × 5.5 cm) on white paper and cut them out.

2 Draw three lines spaced $^1/_8$ in. (3 mm) apart over the entire height of a fuchsia paper, then cut out these strips.

3 Stack them and cut every $2^3/_8$ in. (6 cm).

4 Glue four strips on each rectangle, spacing them about $^1/_8$ in. (3 mm) apart, then cut off the excess.

5 Glue the towels to the ground as in the photo.

1   Trace the pool patterns. Transfer them to the corresponding papers and then cut them out.

    Tip: Make sure to transfer the shadow of the buoy to a different blue than the pool water.

2   Run the blunt edge of the blade along the folding lines. Erase the lines and mark the folds.

3   Glue the two triangular tabs at the corners of the pool to the nearest parts, making sure they are on the outside.

4   Position the pool shadow and the buoy shadow, then the white lines at the bottom of the pool (as indicated on the pattern) and glue.

    Tip: Glue your elements to the bottom of the pool.

5   Fold the pool tabs so that they are outside the pool.

6   Turn your pink-tiled floor over on the back, then glue the pool tabs around the openwork rectangle. Press until the glue is dry.

7   Turn around and glue the edge of the pool.

8   Slide the top tabs of the ladder under the edge of the pool. Glue them together, then glue both remaining strips onto the shade of the pool.

    Tip: Color the visible tabs blue so that they blend into the pool shade.

9   Cut three pieces of toothpicks ⁹⁄₁₆ in. (1.5 cm) long, then glue them vertically with a glue gun under the buoy. Hold them until the glue dries, then glue them to the bottom of the pool.

FOR MORE REALISM

Color the toothpicks blue.

ASSEMBLY

Glue the underside of the pool and the floor strips to the bottom of the Polaroid frame.

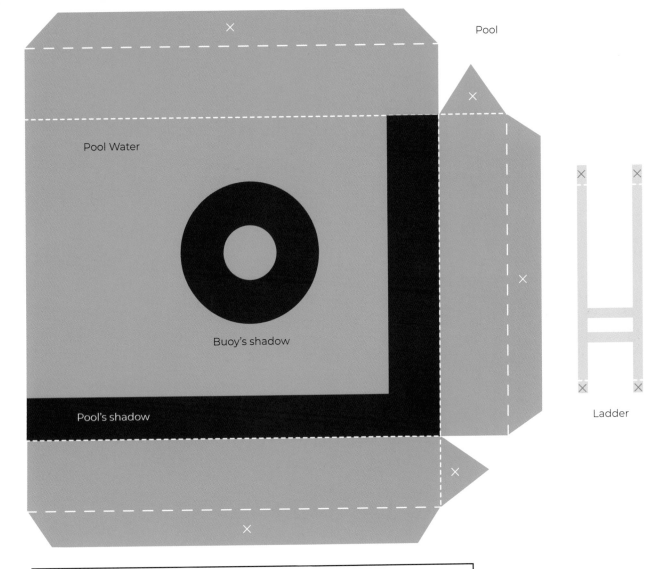

Pool

Pool Water

Buoy's shadow

Pool's shadow

Ladder

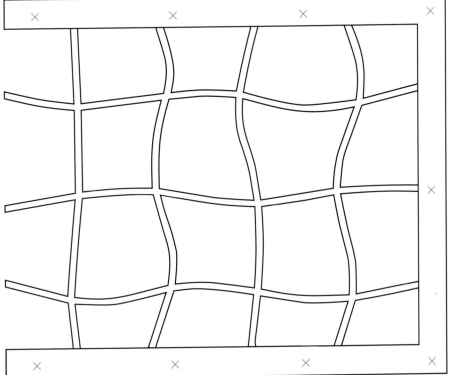

Buoy

Edge and bottom
of the pool

THE UMBRELLAS

1 Trace the pattern of the umbrella. On fuchsia paper, transfer the umbrella once open and twice closed and then cut them out.

2 Run the blunt edge of the blade along the folding lines. Erase the lines.

3 Mark the folds, in the same direction for the open umbrella, and fan shaped for closed umbrellas (see "Specific Techniques: Fold In and Fold Out," p. 16).

4 Glue the tab to the nearest part.

5 For the umbrella base, insert a toothpick at the intersection of the folds. Cut the excess on the high point of the umbrella and glue it if necessary.

6 With the compass, make holes in the "tiled" floor to insert the umbrellas.

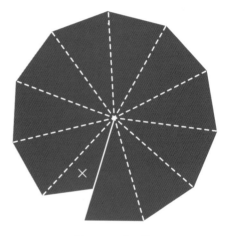

Open umbrella

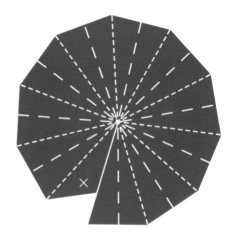

Closed umbrella

THE PLANTS

1 Trace the patterns of the palm trees and foliage. Transfer the palm trees twice on antique-green paper, the foliage four times on khaki-green paper, and cut them out.

2 Cut one of the foliage pieces in half in the height direction.

3 Using the photographs and markings on the pattern (see p. 68), insert the plants into the slots of the Polaroid frame (as shown in step 4 on p. 66).

FOR MORE REALISM

Use different green papers.

Leaves

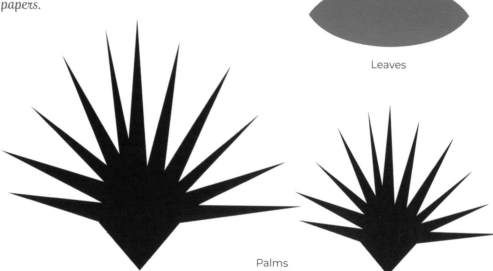

Palms

INSTALLATION

Hammer the nail into the wall and place the Polaroid's hanging hole on the nail. You can also simply display it on a piece of furniture.

BABY'S BEDROOM

Whale Piggy Bank

Lunar Decoration

Llama Mobile

WHALE PIGGY BANK

This baby whale is just waiting to be washed up in the room of a little boy or girl. But first, you'll have to be patient and precise when gluing.

MATERIALS

* Basic kit (see pp. 10–11)
* 2 sheets (letter size):
    - White × 1
    - Blue × 1
* Tracing paper
* Black felt-tip pen
* Blue felt-tip pen
* Old calendar

PAPER (185 gsm unless otherwise indicated)

Body
● Midnight blue

Belly
○ White (160 gsm) (my example uses Canson Midtones paper)

PATTERN KEY

———— cutting line

········ folding line (outward angle)

— — — folding line (inward angle)

✕ gluing area

✚ where to insert the jets of water

DIMENSIONS

Whale piggy bank: 7⅞ × 3¹⁵⁄₁₆ in. (20 × 10 cm)

THE JETS OF WATER

1   Trace the water jet patterns, transfer
them to the tracing paper (see "Basic
Techniques: Reproducing a Pattern,"
p. 12), then cut them out.

2   Color drops with the blue felt-tip pen
on each shape and allow to dry.

3   Overlay the three jets, placing the
largest in the middle. Attach the part
under the dots with tape and fold.

Jets of water

BELLY AND BODY OF THE WHALE

1   Trace the belly and body of the whale, transfer them to
the white and blue paper, respectively, and cut them out.

2   As indicated in the pattern, draw blue lines on the belly
of the whale.

3   Run the blunt edge of the blade along the folding
lines and mark the folds, being careful of their direction
(in or out).

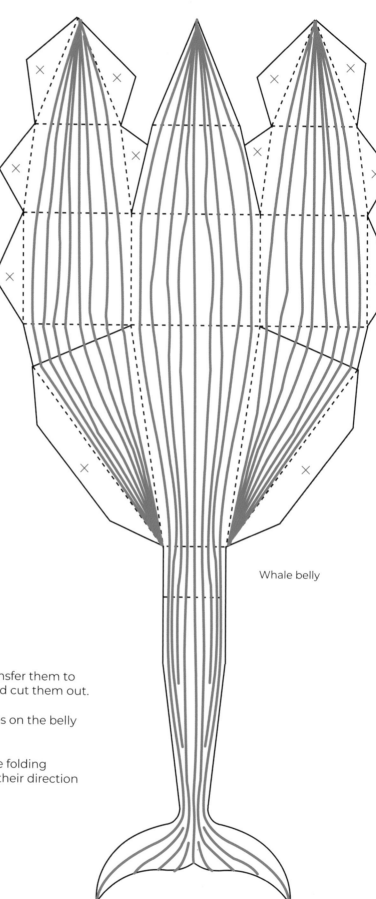

Jets of water

Whale belly

Whale head

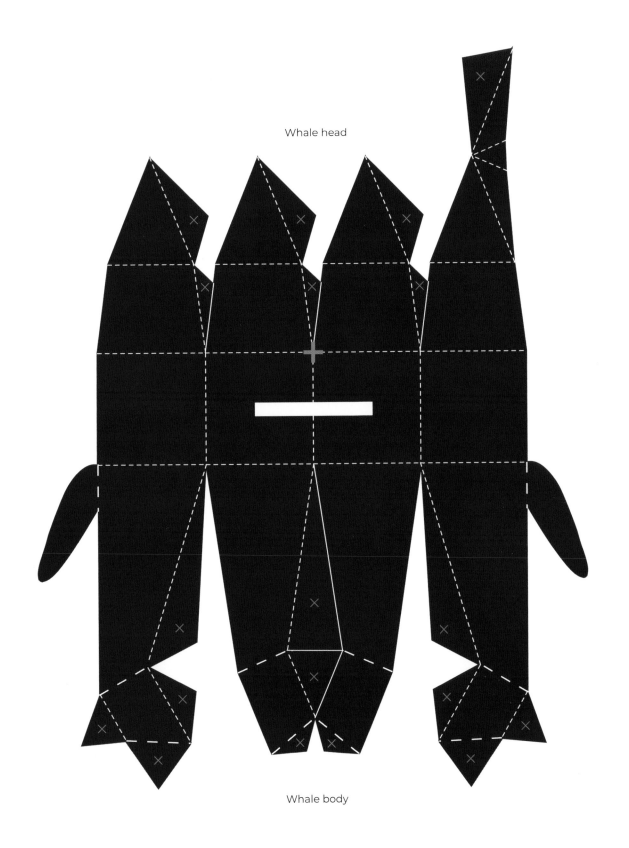

Whale body

MAKING THE HEAD

1 Insert the water jets at the point indicated in the pattern (blue cross on the whale's body) and attach the glued part with adhesive tape to the inside of the whale's body.

2 Glue the body tabs (head side) to the nearest parts, starting with those closest to the slit, then with those that form the tip. Finish by folding down the whale's mouth and glue it (see "Specific Techniques: Rounded Volume," p. 17).

3 Glue the belly tip (head side) to the nearest tabs.

4 Glue the remaining tabs (head side) on the front to insert the belly into the whale's body.

5 Cut out the eyes from the white paper, and color the pupils black. Glue them on each side of the head.

Eyes

MAKING THE TAIL

1 Glue the tabs on the back of the whale, starting with those near the slit. Finish with the ones at the end.

2 Now glue the tail to the end of the back.

3 Glue the two remaining strips of the belly on each side of the whale's back.

4 Finish by sticking the white underside of the tail on the remaining blue tabs and on the tip of the tail.

Tail

LUNAR DECORATION

Immediate departure to infinity and beyond. Building this garland is almost child's play, but it will still require patience when cutting out the elements.

MATERIALS

* Basic kit (see pp. 10–11)
* 8 sheets (letter size):
    - Midnight blue × 1
    - Royal blue × 1
    - Azure blue × 1
    - Red × 1
    - Yellow × 1
    - Orange × 1
    - Light gray × 1
    - Steel gray × 1

* Paper punch (two hole sizes)
* Gold thread
* Thumbtack

PAPER (185 gsm unless otherwise indicated)

Rocket
● Midnight blue ● Royal blue ● Poppy red
● Yellow ● Light gray ● Orange

Planet Saturn
● Midnight blue ● Royal blue ● Yellow

Moon
● Azure blue (160 gsm) ● Light gray ● Steel gray

Stars
● Yellow

PATTERN KEY

———— cutting line

· · · · · · · · folding lne

× gluing area

✛ where to insert the thread

DIMENSIONS

Length: 23⅝ in. (60 cm)

1   Trace the body, wing, and cone patterns of the rocket. Transfer the body and cone of the rocket once to the corresponding papers (midnight blue and poppy red), transfer the wings four times to royal-blue paper, then cut (see "Basic Techniques: Reproducing a Pattern," p. 12).

2   Run the back of the blade on the folding lines of the rocket, cone, and wings. Erase the lines and then mark the folds (see "Basic Techniques: Folding," p. 13).

3   Insert the wings into the slots of the rocket body and glue them.

4   Form the body tube by gluing the large tab on the opposite side and glue the triangular tabs on the octagon.

5   Cut 3⁹⁄₃₂ in. (1 cm) of gold thread. Attach it to the tip of the rocket and tape it down, making sure it is not too visible. Place the cone of the rocket tip upward, with the folds facing you. Pass the lower end of the thread to the tip and secure it with the tape.

6   Form the nose cone by sticking the large tab on the opposite side and stick the triangular tabs on the octagon.

7   Glue the remaining tabs of the rocket body to the octagon of the nose.

8   Trace the pattern of the rocket flame and transfer its outline to yellow paper. Transfer the outline of the orange flame twice and the red flame twice to the corresponding papers and then cut them out.

9   Glue the orange flames on either side of the yellow flame and glue the red flame on top.

10 For the portholes, cut two yellow circles ¹³⁄₁₆ in. (2 cm) in diameter and two light-gray circles ⁹⁄₁₆ in. (1.5 cm) in diameter.

11 Glue the gray circles onto the yellow circles.

12 Insert the flames into the slot of the octagon of the rocket body. Finish by gluing the two portholes on both sides of the rocket and in the extension of the flames.

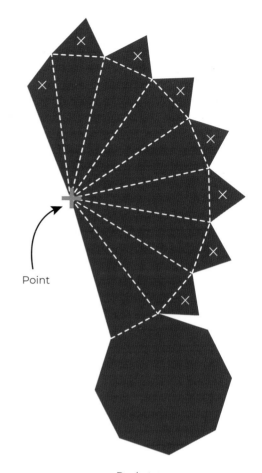

Point

Rocket nose cone

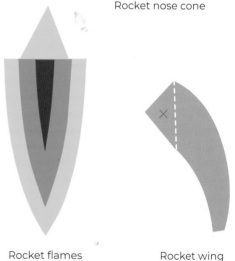

Rocket flames

Rocket wing

Rocket porthole

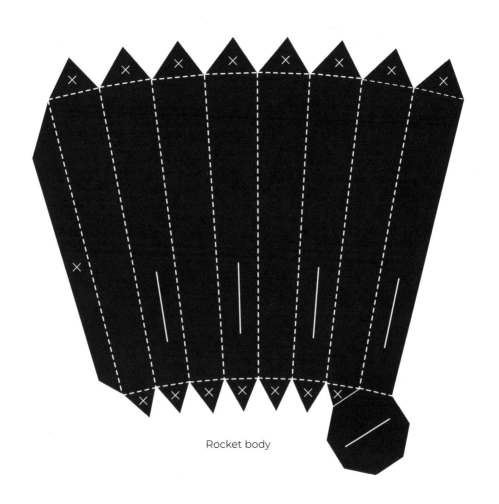

Rocket body

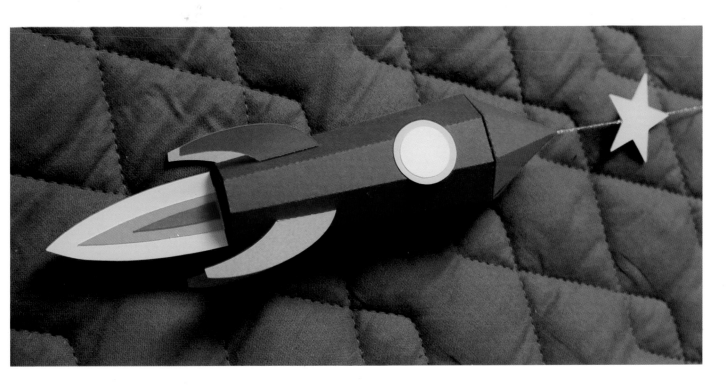

THE PLANET SATURN

1 Trace the patterns of the planet Saturn. Transfer the circle of the planet twice on royal-blue paper, transfer the small rings twice on midnight-blue paper, and transfer the large ring once on yellow paper. Cut them out.

2 Glue four blue rings onto one of the circles of the planet, as shown in the photo, and do the same for the other circle.

3 Glue the yellow ring, as shown on the pattern, then glue it on one of the two planets. Put to one side.

Saturn and its blue rings

Small star

Medium star

Saturn's ring

Large star

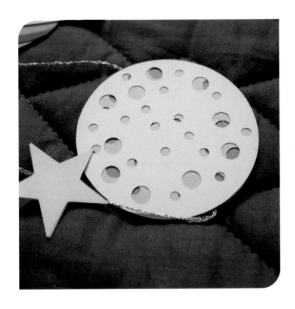

THE STARS

1   Cut eight 1⁹⁄₁₆ × 1⁹⁄₁₆ in. (4 × 4 cm) squares out of the yellow paper.

2   Trace the patterns of the stars and transfer each one to a square.

3   Make three piles (four squares, two squares, two squares). Place the pattern of the medium-sized star on the pile of four squares and the other two patterns on the other two piles.

4   Hold a pile together with your fingers and cut out the stars. Repeat this for each stack. Set them aside.

THE MOON

1   Draw six circles 2⅜ in. (6 cm) in diameter: two in azure blue, two in light gray, and two in steel gray. Cut them out.

2   Overlay your azure-blue circles on your light-gray circles.

3   Make holes of different sizes with the paper punch.

Tip: If you do not have a paper punch, make holes with the tip of the compass and insert your pencil tip to obtain the desired size.

4   Glue an azure-blue circle on a light-gray circle, then glue them on the steel-gray circle. Do the same for the other three circles. Put to one side. To make the contrast for the moon, shift the holes of the blue and light-gray circles.

Azure-blue moon

Light-gray moon

Steel-gray moon

ASSEMBLY

1   At 1⁹⁄₁₆ in. (4 cm) from the rocket, glue the gold thread on a medium star, then glue a second star on the back to hide the thread.

2   At 1⁹⁄₁₆ in. (4 cm) from this star, stick the thread on the back of a moon and proceed as before.

3   At 2⅜ in. (6 cm), stick the thread on the back of the planet Saturn (without yellow ring) with adhesive tape, making sure that the blue rings are in the right direction. Insert Saturn without a ring on the back of Saturn with a ring, then glue.

4   At 1⁹⁄₁₆ in. (4 cm) from Saturn, stick the gold thread on a small star and attach the second one on the back to hide the thread.

5   At 1⁹⁄₁₆ in. (4 cm) from the small star, proceed in the same way for the medium star.

6   At 1⁹⁄₁₆ in. (4 cm) from the medium star, finish in the same way with a large star.

INSTALLATION

Adjust the thread according to the height of your ceiling, tie a knot around a thumbtack, and attach it to the ceiling. You can also hang this mobile against the wall.

LLAMA MOBILE

Use a cloud hanger to make a mobile with llama charm.
The hardest part is gluing the llama. The rest is very simple.

MATERIALS

- ✳ Basic kit (see pp. 10–11)
- ✳ 8 sheets (letter size):
  - Blue × 1
  - White × 1
  - Fuchsia × 1
  - Green × 1
  - Red × 1
  - Burgundy × 1
  - Orange × 1
  - Yellow × 1

- ✳ Large needle
- ✳ Cloud hanger (11¹³⁄₁₆ in. [30 cm] long)
- ✳ Toothpicks
- ✳ Gold-green yarn (or other color)
- ✳ Fishing line
- ✳ Thumbtack
- ✳ Black felt-tip pen

PAPER (185 gsm unless otherwise indicated)

Llama
○ White ● Fuchsia ○ Azure blue (160 gsm)

Cactus
● Antique green ● Fuchsia

Mountain
○ White ● Fuchsia

Circles
● Poppy red ● Burgundy ● Orange

Pom-poms
○ Yellow (120 g)

PATTERN KEY

——— cutting line

········ folding lne

✕ gluing area

✛ where to insert the thread

DIMENSIONS

Hanger + mobile: 11¹³⁄₁₆ × 23⅝ in.
(30 × 60 cm)

THE CIRCLES

1 Cut out fourteen squares of 1³⁄₁₆ × 1³⁄₁₆ in.
   (3 × 3 cm) (six red poppy, four orange, and four
   burgundy).

2 Make three piles, then draw a circle of 1³⁄₁₆ in.
   (2 cm) diameter on the top square.

3 Hold a pile together with your fingers,
   then cut them out. Repeat this for each stack.
   Put to one side.

THE POM-POMS

1 Cut out three 1⁹⁄₁₆ × 5⅛ in. (4 × 13 cm)
   yellow strips.

2 On one of the strips, draw a line at ⅜ in. (1 cm)
   from the edge lengthwise.

3 Stack the three strips, hold firmly, and cut the
   width every ³⁄₁₆ in. (5 mm) approximately up to
   the line previously drawn.

4 Cut three 15¾ in. (40 cm) pieces of yarn. Attach
   the end of the thread on the top of the strip
   with glue, as indicated on the pattern. Roll the
   band of paper very tightly around the yarn. Glue
   the end of the strip. Repeat these steps for the
   other two yellow pom-poms.

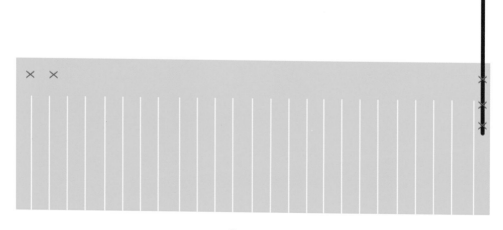

Pom-pom

THE CACTUS

1   Trace the three patterns of the cactus and the flower. Transfer each side of the cactus once to the antique-green paper, the flower twice to the fuchsia paper, and cut them out (see "Basic Techniques: Reproducing a Pattern," p. 12).

2   Run the back of the blade along the folding lines. Erase the lines, then mark the folds (see "Basic Techniques: Folding," p. 13).

3   Glue the A side of cactus 1 to the A side of cactus 2.

4   Glue the B side of cactus 1 to the B side of cactus 3.

5   At 1³⁄₁₆ in. (3 cm) from a pom-pom, stick the thread on a red circle and attach a second circle to hide the thread.

6   At 1³⁄₁₆ in. (3 cm) from the circle, insert the yarn between the two sides C of the cactus before sticking them together.

7   Glue the flower on the part of the thread that protrudes from the top of the cactus, then attach the second one to hide the thread. Put it to one side.

Cactus flower

Cactus 1

Cactus 2

Cactus 3

THE MOUNTAIN

1 Trace the mountain pattern. Transfer the outline twice to white paper and the bottom of the mountain twice to fuchsia paper.

2 Glue a fuchsia mountain on a white mountain. Repeat this a second time.

3 At 2 in. (5 cm) from one of the pom-poms, stick the thread on an orange circle, then attach a second circle to hide the thread.

4 At 2 in. (5 cm) from the orange circle, attach the thread to the back of one of the mountains with glue and attach the second one to hide the thread. Put it aside.

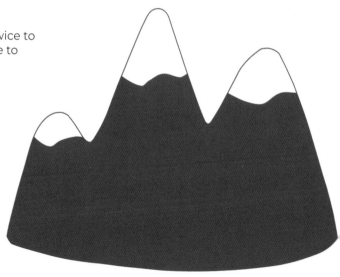

Mountain
(1 × white, 1 × fuchsia)

THE LLAMA BODY

1 Trace the llama's patterns (pp. 95 and 96). Transfer them to the corresponding papers.

2 Run the back of your blade along the folding lines. Erase the lines, then mark the folds according to the instructions on the pattern, and be careful with the folding direction.

3 With the tip of the compass, make the holes indicated on the body pattern (see "Basic Techniques: Making a Hole," p. 13). Expand them with a toothpick.

4 Start by gluing the tabs indicated by the arrows on the body pattern and continue with the next ones.

5 Glue the widest end of the strip to the tip of the central band. Glue together the remaining tabs under this strip.

6 Insert the tail into the indicated slot on the body pattern.

7 Draw the eyes and mouth on the head of the llama with the black felt-tip pen.

8 Glue the tabs of the head under the strip, as indicated on the template.

9 Glue the remaining tabs of the head onto the body of the llama.

Central band

Llama tail

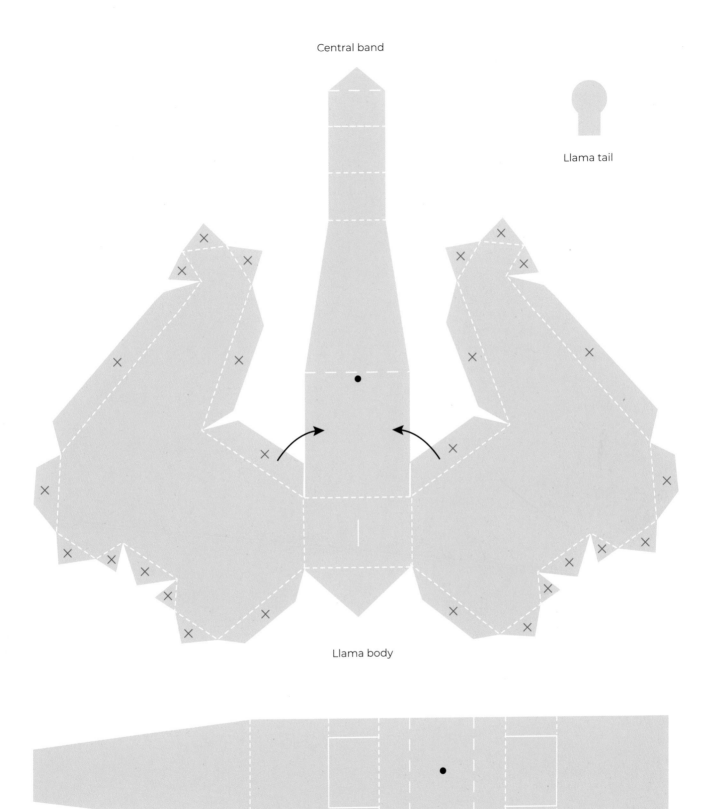

Llama body

Llama body band

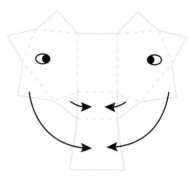

Llama head

× 2   × 2

Llama ears

Blanket

10 Color the tips of the legs with a black felt-tip pen.

11 Glue the tiny tabs of the legs to the nearest parts.

12 Lift the rectangles on the body. Insert the legs and fold down the rectangles.

13 Cut out and glue the white ears onto the blue ears (the outgoing fold must be on the blue side). Stick them onto the llama's head.

14 Cut out, fold, and secure the blanket on the back of the llama, leaving the hole previously made visible.

15 At ¹³⁄₁₆ in. (2 cm) from the last pom-pom, stick the yarn on a burgundy circle and glue on a second circle to hide the yarn.

16 Make a knot ³⁄₁₆ in. (5 cm) from the circle, and using the needle, pass the thread through the body of the llama.

   Tip: If your needle is too small, attach the yarn to the end of a toothpick.

17 Remove the needle, stick the thread on a red circle 3⅛ in. (8 cm) from the llama, and then glue on a second circle to hide the yarn. Set it aside.

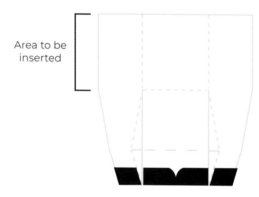

Area to be inserted

Front legs

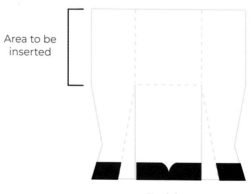

Area to be inserted

Back legs

ASSEMBLY

1   Tie the cactus thread on the left of the cloud hanger and 1⁹⁄₁₆ in. (4 cm) from the flower. Make a double knot and cut off the excess. Glue a burgundy circle on either side of the hanger to hide the knot.

2   Tie the llama thread in the center of the cloud hanger and 2¾ in. (7 cm) from the red circle. Make a double knot and cut off the excess. Glue an orange circle on either side of the hanger as before.

3   Tie the mountain thread on the right of the cloud hanger and ⅜ in. (6 cm) from the mountain. Make a double knot and cut off the excess. Glue a red circle on either side of the hanger to finish.

INSTALLATION

Hang some fishing line on the hanger hook. Adjust the thread according to the height of your ceiling and tie a knot around a thumbtack to hang the mobile. You can also let it hang against a wall.

PARENTS' BEDROOM

Parrot Mirror

Peacock Headboard

PARROT MIRROR

Create a tropical atmosphere with simple folds and very little gluing! Leaves and a parrot to decorate a mirror, or to detach and use for a special event.

MATERIALS

＊ Basic kit (see pp. 10–11)

＊ 7 sheets (letter size):

- Forest green × 1
- Antique green × 1
- Turquoise green × 1
- Midnight blue × 1
- Royal blue × 1
- Azure blue × 1
- Yellow × 1

＊ Mirror and nail (optional)

＊ Glue gun

＊ Double-sided adhesive tape

＊ Green sewing thread

PAPER (185 gsm unless otherwise indicated)

Parrot
● Midnight blue ● Royal blue ● Yellow
○ Azure blue (160 gsm))

Banana leaves
● Antique green ● Forest green

Palm leaves
● Antique green ● Mint green

Falling leaves
● Antique green ● Forest green ● Mint green

PATTERN SCALE 1

PATTERN KEY

—— cutting line

········· folding line (outward angle)

— — — folding line (inward angle)

✕ gluing area

DIMENSIONS

Mirror: 11¹³⁄₁₆ in. (30 cm) diameter

THE PARROT

THE BODY

1. Trace the patterns of the parrot's crest, body, head, and beak. Transfer them to the corresponding papers, then cut them out. Don't forget the slit in the body (see "Basic Techniques: Reproducing a Pattern," p. 12).

2. Glue the crest to the top of the parrot's body, then the azure-blue head onto the back of the body. Be sure to align the shapes properly.

3. Glue the smallest beak to the other, aligning them properly.

4. Glue it to the front of the parrot's head.

5. Glue the upper part of the slot to the lower part (see "Specific Techniques: Half Volume," p. 16).

THE WING

1. Trace the wing patterns. Transfer them to the corresponding papers and cut them out.

2. Run the back of your blade along the folding lines. Erase the lines, then mark the folds (see "Basic Techniques: Folding," p. 13).

3. Glue the top of the royal-blue wing under the midnight-blue wing according to the areas to be glued. Do the same for the azure-blue wing, gluing it under the royal-blue wing.

4. Glue the left part of the slot of the dark-blue wing to the right part.

5. Glue the wing to the body, aligning the points.

Parrot crest

Parrot body

Parrot beak

Parrot head

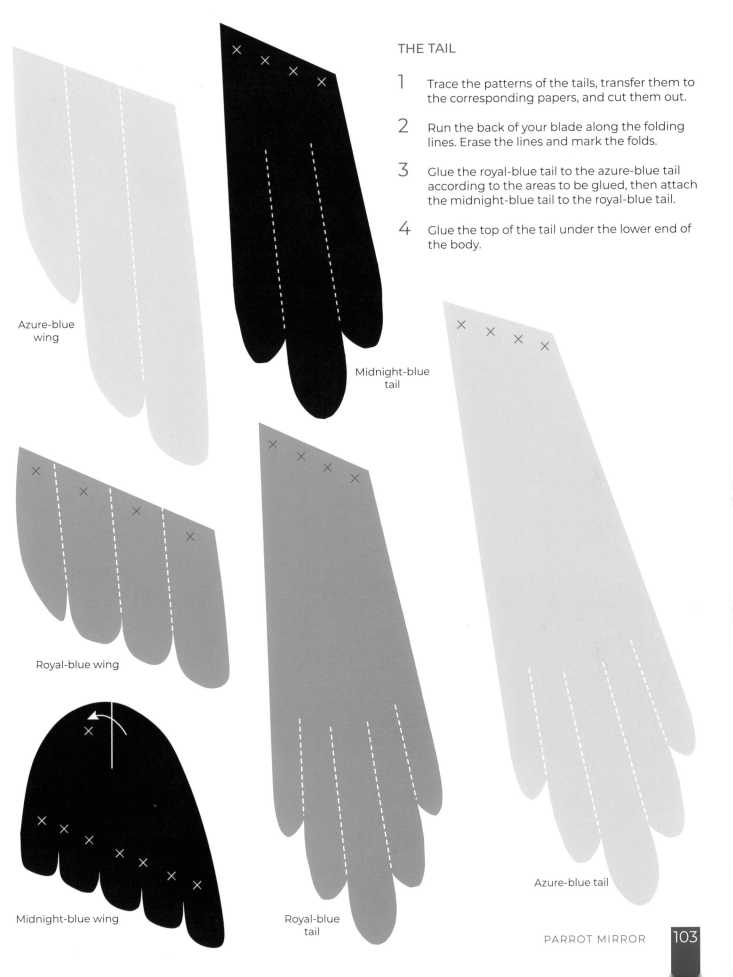

Azure-blue wing

Midnight-blue tail

Royal-blue wing

Midnight-blue wing

Royal-blue tail

Azure-blue tail

THE TAIL

1   Trace the patterns of the tails, transfer them to the corresponding papers, and cut them out.

2   Run the back of your blade along the folding lines. Erase the lines and mark the folds.

3   Glue the royal-blue tail to the azure-blue tail according to the areas to be glued, then attach the midnight-blue tail to the royal-blue tail.

4   Glue the top of the tail under the lower end of the body.

THE LEVES

BANANA LEAVES

1   Trace the three banana leaves. Transfer leaves 1 and 2 once, and leaf 3 twice, to the corresponding papers, and then cut them out.

2   Run the back of your blade along the folding lines. Erase the lines and mark the folds.

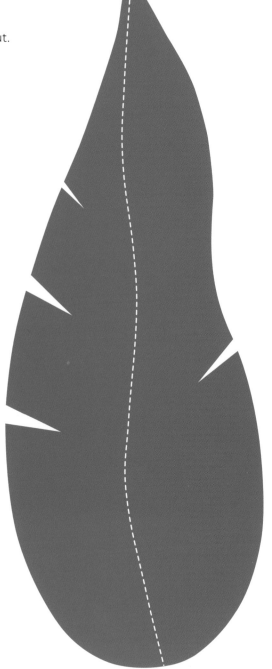

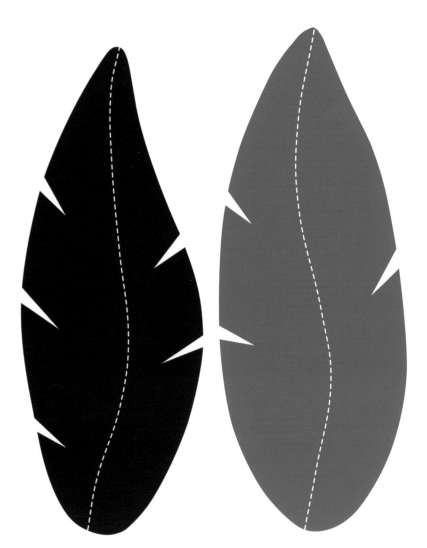

Banana leaf 2   Banana leaf3   Banana leaf 1

Palm leaf 1

Palm leaf 2

PALM LEAVES

1 Trace the patterns of the palm leaves. Transfer palm leaf 1 and palm leaf 2 to the corresponding papers once, and cut them out.

2 Run the back of your blade along the folding lines. Erase the lines and mark the folds as if making a fan (see "Specific Techniques: "Fold In and Fold Out," p. 16).

3 Tighten the folds together again, like a fan.

FALLING LEAVES

1 Turn on your glue gun.

2 Draw four circles 1⁹⁄₁₆ in. (4 cm) in diameter on the three green papers. You will get twelve circles.

3 Cut along the outlines, making wavy lines with your scissors.

4 Cut a slit to the center and glue the left side of the slit to the right side.

5 Enlarge the hole in the center of the leaves with a toothpick.

6 Cut four lengths of 7⅞ in. (20 cm) green thread and then tie a knot at the end of each one for the flower pistil.

7 Run the threads through the mint-green leaves by placing the knots inside the leaf.

8 Insert the forest-green leaves at ⁹⁄₁₆ or ¹³⁄₁₆ in. (1.5 or 2 cm) from the turquoise-green leaves, then put a point of glue inside the leaf.

Tip: Vary the spacing for each length of thread.

9 Finish with the antique-green leaves.

Mint green leaf

Forest green leaf

Antique green leaf

ASSEMBLY

1 Attach the large banana leaf to the mirror with double-sided adhesive tape, as shown in the photo.

2 Glue the banana leaf #2 to the right of the large banana leaf. Glue leaf #3 under the mirror and to the left of the large banana leaf.

3 Attach the palm leaf #1 to the leaves of the banana tree with glue, then both palm leaves #2.

4 Attach the parrot with double-sided adhesive tape.

5 Finish by gluing the ends of the threads of falling leaves onto the back of the mirror with tape.

INSTALLATION

Hang your mirror on a nail.

PEACOCK HEADBOARD

Before you luxuriate in beauty in your very own bed, use your creative energy to cut out these peacock feathers.

MATERIALS

* Basic kit (see pp. 10–11)

* 6 sheets (format 19¹¹⁄₁₆ × 27⁹⁄₁₆ in. [50 × 70 cm]):
  - Antique green × 3
  - Mint green × 3

* 7 sheets (letter size):
  - Forest green × 3
  - Gold × 2
  - Midnight blue × 1
  - Royal blue × 1

* Stiff paper sheet (minimum 250 gsm)

* Glue spray can

* Glue gun

* Adhesive picture hangers

* Masking tape

* Repositionable sticky tack (Blu-tack or similar)

PAPER (185 gsm unless otherwise indicated)

Base of the feathers

● Antique green   ○ Mint green (270 gsm)

Details of the feathers

● Antique green (270 gsm)   ● Forest green
● Royal blue   ● Midnight blue
● Frosted gold (150 gsm) (my example is Daler-Rowney Canford paper)

PATTERN KEY

──────── cutting line

················ construction line

DIMENSIONS

Headboard: 59¹⁄₁₆ × 36⁷⁄₁₆ in. (150 × 90 cm)

9 feathers for a 47¼ in. (120 cm) wide bed; for wider beds, add feathers

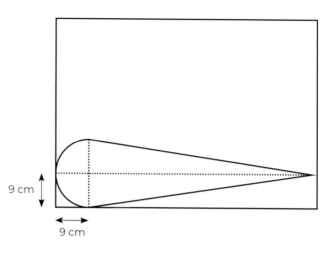

Figure 1

BASE OF THE FEATHERS

1　Place an antique-green sheet of paper 19¹¹⁄₁₆ × 27⁹⁄₁₆ in. (50 × 70 cm) in landscape format.

2　As in figure 1, draw a line at 3⁹⁄₁₆ in. (9 cm) from the edge along the entire length of the leaf.

3　Make a mark on this line 3⁹⁄₁₆ in. (9 cm) from the left edge of the sheet.

4　With the square, draw a perpendicular line at the bottom of the sheet and passing through this mark.

5　Place the tip of the compass on this mark, then draw a semicircle 7¹⁄₁₆ in. (18 cm) in diameter to the left edge of the sheet.

6　Close the semicircle by drawing a triangle, as shown in figure 1, and then cut out the feather.

7　Transfer it as shown in figure 2 to the other sheets of the same size, in order to have nine antique-green feathers and nine mint-green feathers in total, and cut them out.

8　Trace the patterns A and B of the feathers (see pp. 113 and 114). Transfer them to the corresponding papers and then cut them out (see "Basic Techniques: Reproducing a Pattern," p. 12).

9　Place them on an antique-green sheet of paper in the order shown in figure 3 (from the drop to the small arrow; see p. 111). Trace all of the outlines.

10　Draw two lines in the height to connect the drop on pattern B to the arrows on pattern A (see figure 3 on p. 111).

11　Cut out the outlines of this shape with a cutter.

12　Overlay this feather on an antique-green feather and trace the outlines to be cut out. Repeat this on another antique-green feather.

Figure 2

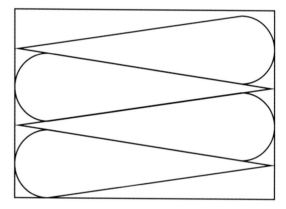

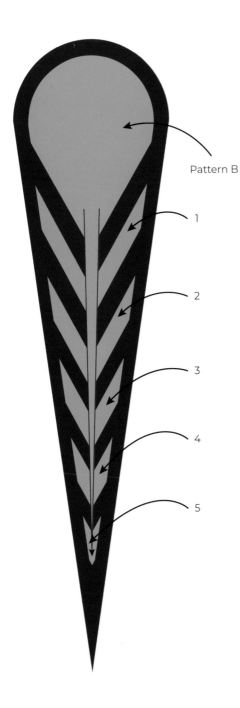

Pattern B

1

2

3

4

5

Figure 3
(not to scale)

13 Make a pile of four and another of three antique-green feathers. Place the feathers shown in step 12 above each stack.

14 Attach them with pieces of masking tape so that they do not move.

15 Use the cutter on the marked outlines.

16 Remove the adhesive tapes.

17 Cover the cutout antique-green feathers with spray glue and glue them to the mint-green feathers.

Tip: Spray outside and on protective cardboard.

Pattern A

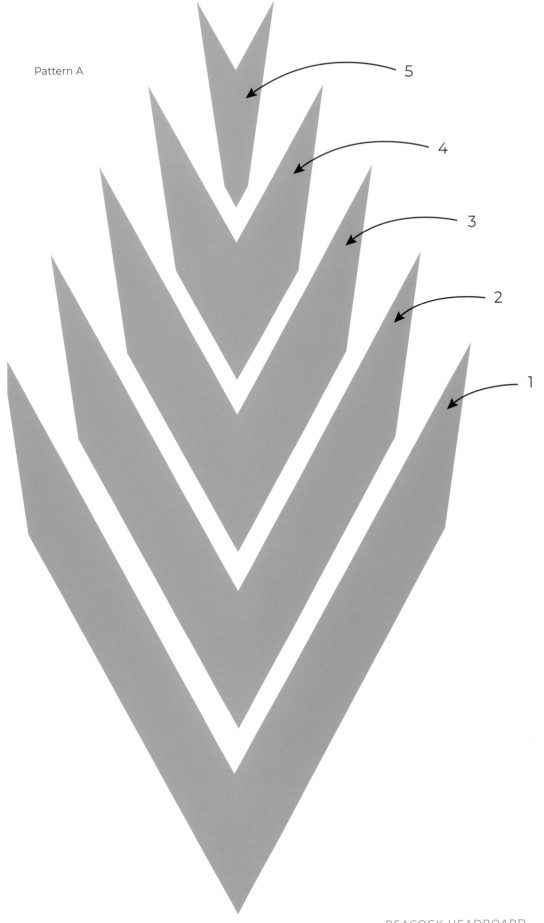

5

4

3

2

1

Feather details

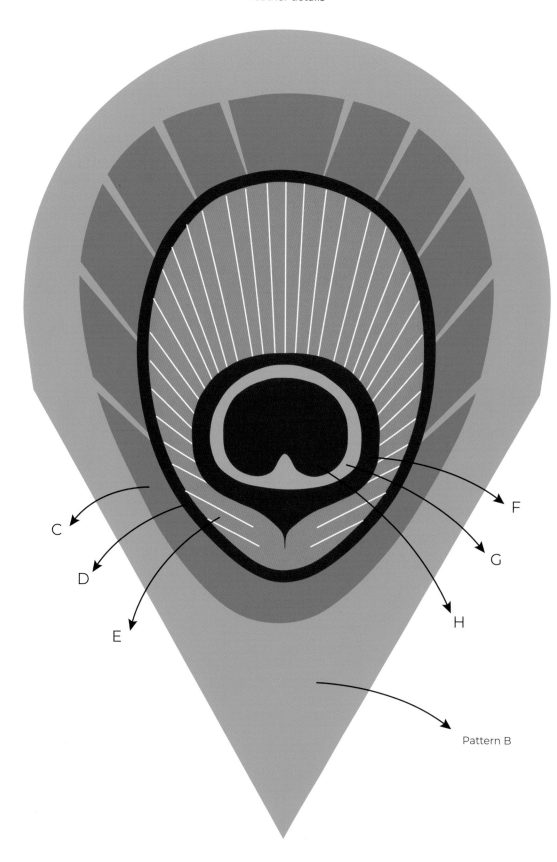

C

D

E

F

G

H

Pattern B

FEATHER DETAILS

1. Trace patterns C, D, E, F, G, and H. Transfer them nine times each to the corresponding papers. Cut out the outlines, and then on the inner cutting lines of E.

2. Glue H to G, G to F, F to E, E to D, and D to C.

3. With your finger, bend some strips of gold paper.

4. Glue all these details on the base of each feather.

Figure 4
(gluing order for the feathers, not to scale)

INSTALLATION

1. Place the sticky tack on the back of each feather at each end.

2. Stick them to your wall, using figure 4 for the order in which the feathers are attached.

3. Peel off a feather, replace the sticky tack with an adhesive picture hanger, then stick it back on. Repeat this for each feather.

THE GARDEN

Potted Plants

Tropical Cabins

Flower Wreath

POTTED PLANTS

No more watering—create your easy-care paper plants!
As with real ones, all you need to grow them will be a little patience.

MATERIALS

- ✴ Basic kit (see pp. 10–11)
- ✴ 7 or 8 sheets (letter size):

    - Burgundy (× 3)
    - Antique green (× 1 or × 2)
    - Mint green (× 1)
    - Pink (× 1)
    - Brown (× 1) ³⁄₁₆ in. (0.5 cm)

    Thick foam core

- ✴ 4 terra-cotta pots
- ✴ Cutting pliers for wire
- ✴ Glue gun
- ✴ Large needle
- ✴ Green wire
- ✴ Green string
- ✴ 9 skewers

PAPER (180 gsm)

Oxalis butterfly plant
● Burgundy

Ceropegia
● Antique green

Begonia rex
● Mint green ● Burgundy

Calathea
● Light pink ● Burgundy ● Mint green
● Antique green

PATTERN KEY

PATTERN SCALE 1

——— cutting line

········ folding line

✕ gluing area

● hole

DIMENSIONS

2 terra-cotta pots, 2¾ in. (7 cm) diameter

2 terra-cotta pots, 3⁹⁄₁₆ in. (9 cm) diameter

OXALIS BUTTERFLY PLANT

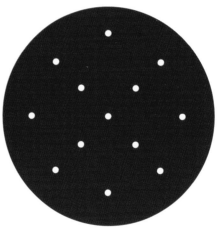

1   Trace the pattern of the triangles strip. Transfer it to the width of your burgundy sheet, then cut out the strip alone.

2   Transfer this strip three more times, cut them, and then stack them by placing the one with the triangles on top.

3   Hold the strips together between your fingers and cut out the triangles.

4   Trace the pattern of the leaf and transfer it to eight triangles (see "Basic Techniques: Reproducing a Pattern," p. 12).

5   Make eight piles by placing the traced leaves on top of the stacks.

6   Hold a pile together between your fingers and round the edges with scissors. Repeat this with the other piles.

7   Run the back of your blade along in the middle of each triangle and then fold them in half (see "Basic Techniques: Folding," p. 13).

8   With the needle, make a hole on the side of the inward angle (valley fold) (see mark on the leaf pattern).

9   Turn on your glue gun.

10 Cut twelve 5⅛ in. (13 cm) wire rods.

11 Thread a first leaf onto the end of the stem and put a spot of glue (with the glue gun) under the leaf.

12 Thread a second leaf ³⁄₁₆ in. (0.5 cm) from the first one, turn it so that the edges align, then glue it in place. Continue in the same way for the third leaf.

13 Repeat steps 11 and 12 for the twelve remaining stems.

Leaf

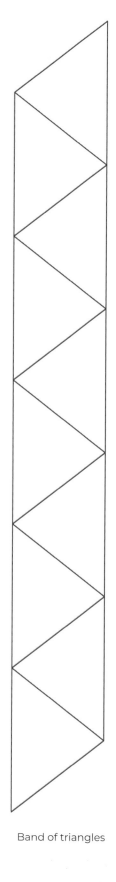

Band of triangles

Soil

1   Trace the two patterns of the begonia leaves. Transfer them nine times to the corresponding papers.

2   Cut them out, making waves with your scissors on the outlines of the underside and top of the leaves.

3   Glue the green leaves onto the burgundy leaves.

4   Give volume to the leaves by sticking the part on the left of the slit onto the right (see "Specific Techniques: Half Volume," p. 16).

5   Insert a skewer at the top of the slit. Put a dot of glue underneath the leaves if necessary.

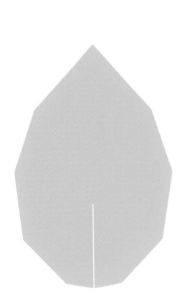

Top of leaf

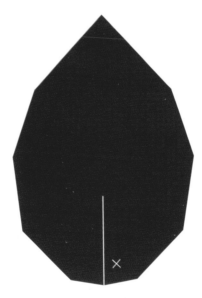

Underside of leaf

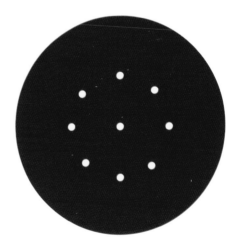

Soil

CALATHEA

1 Trace the base of the leaf, transfer it nine times on light-pink paper and nine times on burgundy paper, and then cut them out.

2 Run the back of your blade along the folding lines and mark the folds.

Tip: To save time, cut rectangles $1^3/_{16} \times 3^{15}/_{16}$ in. (3 × 10 cm) and make three stacks. Transfer the pattern to the top rectangle. Hold the pile firmly and then cut out the leaves. Mark the folds with the back of your blade in the middle of each leaf.

3 Trace the patterns of the leaves, transfer them twice each to the corresponding papers, and cut them out.

4 Run the back of your blade along the folding lines, then mark the folds.

5 Glue the antique-green leaves onto the mint-green leaves, then onto the light-pink bases.

6 On your sheet of burgundy paper, draw ten lines along the entire length, spacing them $^3/_{16}$ in. (0.5 cm) apart.

7 Run the back of your blade along every other line. Cut out the other lines.

8 Fold and glue the inside.

Tip: For more support, insert a wire rod before sticking.

9 Cut these rods into two equal lengths.

10 Glue the end of these rods to the rounded bases of the burgundy leaves.

11 Then glue the pink base onto the burgundy base.

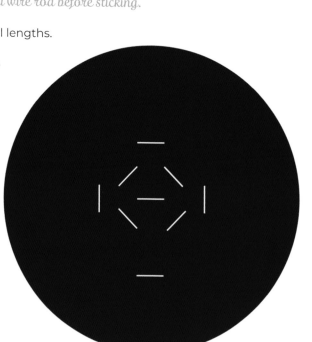

Soil

Bottom leaf
(light pink/burgundy)

Leaf 1   Leaf 2   Leaf 3

CEROPEGIA

1 Draw about sixty 1¾6 × 1¾6 in. (3 × 3 cm) squares on the antique-green paper. To do this, draw a grid over the entire sheet, spacing the lines 1¾6 in. (3 cm) apart.

2 Cut out the strips, stack them, and cut them into squares.

3 Trace the pattern of the Ceropegia leaf (see p. 124). Transfer it to ten squares.

4 Make ten stacks with the squares, placing the traced leaves on the top squares.

5 Hold a pile together between your fingers and cut out the leaves by following the traced line. Repeat this with the other piles.

6 Cut seven lengths of string 11¾6 in. (30 cm) long. Make a knot at the end of each piece.

7 Thread a piece of string through the needle.

8 Make a hole in the leaf and thread it to the knot. Place a second leaf ⅜ in. (1 cm) from the first one. Apply a spot of glue under the leaf.

9 Thread a third leaf at 2 in. (5 cm), glue it, then a fourth one at ⅜ in. (1 cm) and glue it. Repeat this until you have eight leaves on the string.

10 Make four strings of eight leaves and three strings of ten leaves.

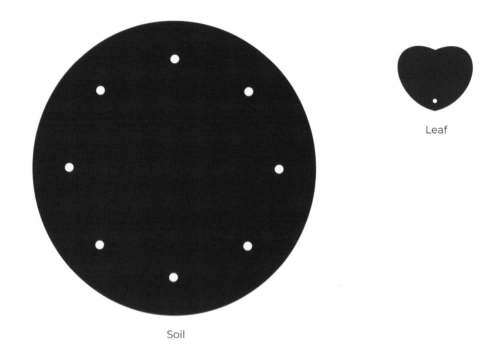

Leaf

Soil

INSTALLATION

1   Trace the four patterns of the soil (see pp. 120, 121, 122 and 124), transfer them to brown paper, then cut out the circles.

2   Glue these brown circles onto the foam core, then cut them out with a cutter. To ensure that the circles fit into the pot, bevel the foam core.

3   With the needle or cutter, make holes in the foam core, as shown on the patterns.

4   For the oxalis, first insert a rod in the center of the foam core and twist the protruding part into waves. Then insert four rods surrounding the first, twist them, and then do the same for the last ones.

5   For the begonia, insert a first rod in the middle of the foam core and insert the others at an angle.

6   For the calathea, insert a first stem in the middle of the foam core, four surrounding it, followed by the last four. Then fold the leaves outward.

7   For the ceropegia, insert the strings with a skewer and attach them with adhesive tape to the underside of the circle.

8   Glue the edges of the foam core circles together before placing them into their corresponding pots.

TROPICAL CABINS

This miniature world requires a gardener's patience for meticulously cutting out the ladders and the terrace.

MATERIALS

* Basic kit (see pp. 10–11)
* 3 sheets (letter size):
  - Pink × 3
* Green plant
* Glue gun
* 12 skewers

PAPER (185 gsm)

Small cabin
◯ Light pink

Large cabin
◯ Light pink

PATTERN
SCALE
1

PATTERN KEY

──────── cutting line

········ folding line

✕   gluing area

●   hole

DIMENSIONS

Terra-cotta pot 7⅞ in. (20 cm) diameter

THE TERRACE

1 Trace the terrace pattern and the large ladder pattern. Transfer them to light-pink paper and cut them out (see "Basic Techniques: Reproducing a Pattern," p. 12).

2 Make four holes in the terrace with the compass.

3 Run the back of your blade along the dotted line. Gently erase the lines and mark the folds (see "Basic Techniques: Folding," p. 13).

4 Glue the four tabs of the terrace to the closest parts.

5 Glue the large ladder to the terrace on a level with the empty space.

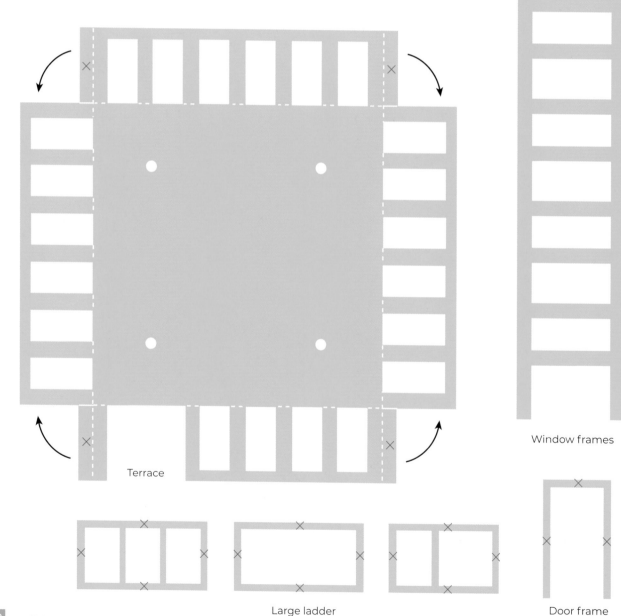

Terrace

Window frames

Large ladder

Door frame

THE CABIN WITH A TERRACE

1   Trace the pattern of the cabin with a terrace and the door and window frames. Transfer them to pink paper.

2   Cut out the outlines first and then the inner elements.

3   With your compass, make a hole in the door, insert the tip of a skewer to enlarge it, then remove it (see "Basic Techniques: Making a Hole," p. 13).

4   Run the back of your blade along the dotted lines around the door. Erase the lines and mark the folds.

5   Form the structure of the cabin by gluing the walls first.

6   Form the roof by gluing the triangular tab to the nearest part. Then glue the base of the triangles to the tabs at the top of each wall.

7   Glue on the door and window frames.

THE ROOF

1   Trace the roof pattern and transfer it four times onto light-pink paper.

2   Cut out according to the indicated marks, without touching the top.

3   Shape it slightly with your nail (see "Basic Techniques: Shaping the Pattern," p. 14).

4   Glue the tip and sides of each triangle to the triangles on the cabin roof, making sure that the pencil lines are not visible.

Cabin terrace

Roof

ASSEMBLING THE CABIN WITH A TERRACE

1. Using adhesive tape, glue a skewer to each inside corner of the cabin.

2. Glue the remaining tabs of the cabin to the terrace.

3. Insert the skewers into the four holes of the terrace.

4. Cut skewers into eight 2⅜ in. (6 cm) sticks, then glue them to the stilts with a glue gun, crossing them over.

THE SMALL CABIN

1 Trace the pattern of the small cabin, window frames, and small ladder. Transfer the ladder and cabin once and the window frame four times.

2 Cut out the outlines first and then the inner elements.

3 With your compass, make a hole in the door, insert the tip of a skewer to enlarge it, and then remove it.

4 Run the back of your blade along the dotted lines and mark the folds.

5 Form the structure of the cabin by first gluing the walls and then the roof.

6 Glue the window frames and then the ladder at the base of the door.

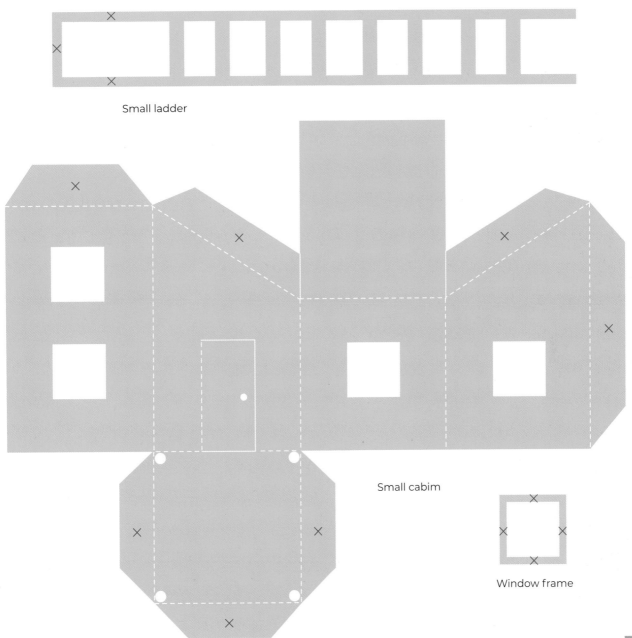

Small ladder

Small cabim

Window frame

SMALL CABIN'S ROOF

Roof

1 Trace the roof pattern and transfer it to light-pink paper.

2 Cut out the rectangle and the inner lines.

3 Shape it slightly with your nail.

4 Glue the crest and sides to the top of the cabin, making sure the pencil lines don't show.

5 Insert skewers at the four corners of the cabin.

INSTALLATION

Place the cabins in your plant. Shorten the ladders and skewers if necessary.

FLOWER WREATH

Tired of wilting flowers? This wreath is the solution to keeping flowers ever fresh in your home. You don't need to have a green thumb, but you do need a careful hand to bring forth ranunculus, anemones, and carnations.

MATERIALS

* Basic kit (see pp. 10–11)
* 8 sheets (letter size):

    - Moss green × 1
    - Antique green × 2
    - Pink × 1
    - Fuchsia × 1
    - Raspberry × 1
    - Blue × 1
    - White × 1

* Gold wire lampshade circle
* Pinking scissors
* Glue gun
* 4 toothpicks
* Nail
* Twine or decorative ribbon

PAPER (185 gsm, unless otherwise indicated)

Ranunculus
● Fuchsia

Ranunculus heart
● Moss green   ● Antique green

Carnations and small ranunculus
● Light pink (160 g)

Pistils
● Duck blue

Anemones
○ White (160 g)

Berries
● Raspberry (160 g)

Foliage
● Antique green

PATTERN
SCALE
1

PATTERN KEY

〰〰〰 cutting line with the pinking scissors

——— cutting line

· · · · · · · folding line

✕ gluing area

DIMENSIONS

Lampshade circle: 8¹¹⁄₁₆ in. (22 cm) diameter

THE RANUNCULUS

1 Turn on your glue gun.

2 Trace the patterns of the ranunculus. Transfer them to the corresponding papers and cut them out (see "Basic Techniques: Reproducing a Pattern," p. 12).

3 Gently erase the lines.

4 Wrap the spiral around itself, starting at the end.

5 Once in the center, apply glue with the gun, as indicated on the patterns.

6 Place the spiral on the glue and press lightly.

7 Cut three strips ⁹⁄₁₆ in. (1.5 cm), ³⁄₈ in. (1 cm), and ³⁄₁₆ in. (0.5 cm) wide along the length of your moss-green and antique-green papers. Sizes vary according to the size of the ranunculus (⁹⁄₁₆ in. [1.5 cm] band for the large ranunculus).

8 Curl these strips with your scissors.

9 Form moss-green cylinders by rolling the paper twice. Cut off the excess paper.

10 Glue the bottom with a glue gun and attach it to the heart of the ranunculus.

11 Repeat this with antique-green paper, making sure that the cylinders are smaller than the moss-green cylinders. Glue them in the center of the previous cylinders.

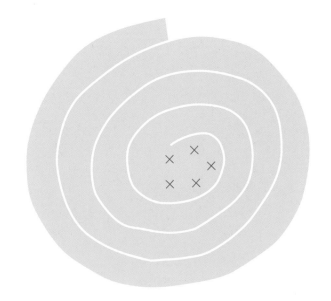

Small pale pink ranunculus

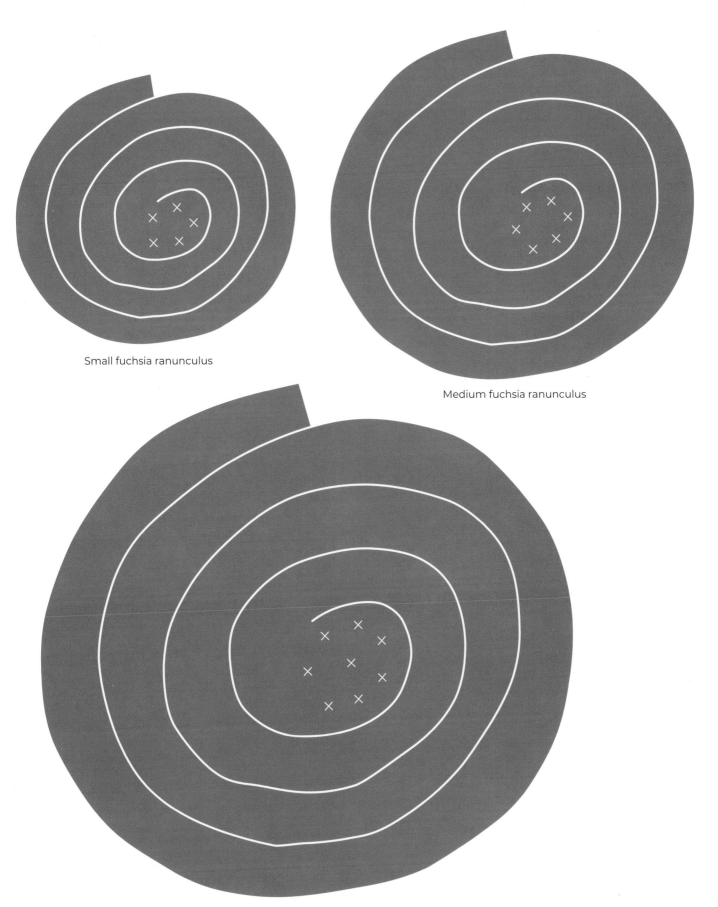

Small fuchsia ranunculus

Medium fuchsia ranunculus

Large fuchsia ranunculus

THE ANEMONES

1   Trace the patterns of the small and large anemones. Transfer them to white paper.

2   Gently erase the lines if necessary.

3   With your ruler, shape the petals (see "Basic Techniques: Shaping the Pattern," p. 14).

4   Glue the petals one on top of the other in descending order, by turning them a quarter circle and shifting them each time.

5   Trace the pistils' patterns. Transfer them to the duck-blue paper and cut them out.

6   Fold the pistils.

7   Glue the small pistil onto the large one.

8   Glue them in the centers of the small and large anemones.

Reproduce this petal 3 times

Reproduce this petal 3 times

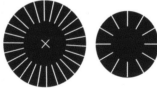

Pistils

THE CARNATIONS

1 Cut two strips 1⁹⁄₁₆ in. (4 cm) wide along the length of your light-pink sheet.

2 On one of the long sides, draw small lines every ¹³⁄₁₆ in. (2 cm).

3 On the other, draw a line at ⅜ in. (1 cm), then every ¹³⁄₁₆ in. (2 cm).

4 With a pencil, join the lines to form triangles, as shown on the pattern.

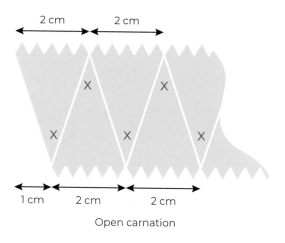

Open carnation

5 Cut the two long sides of the strips with pinking scissors.

6 Then cut the diagonals with flat scissors to obtain forty triangular petals.

7 Gently erase the lines if necessary.

8 Fold them slightly in half in the height direction, then make two piles of sixteen petals (for the two large carnations) and one pile of eight (for the small carnation).

9 Cut the tips off three toothpicks.

10 On the tip of a toothpick, glue the tip of two petals face to face with the glue gun. Slightly crush the petals.

11 Turn your toothpick 45° and glue on two more petals.

12 Repeat this with all the petals from your first pile.

13 Shape the petals to open your carnation.

14 Do the same for the other two carnations.

15 Cut off the excess toothpicks.

THE LEAVES

1 Trace the leaf pattern, transfer it five times to the antique-green paper, and cut them out.

2 Run the back of your blade along the dotted lines. Erase the lines and mark the fold (see "Basic Techniques: Folding," p.13)

Leaf

THE BERRIES

1 Draw twenty-four squares of ⁹⁄₁₆ × ⁹⁄₁₆ in. (1.5 × 1.5 cm) on the raspberry paper. To do this, draw a grid pattern with the lines ⁹⁄₁₆ in. (1.5 cm) apart.

2 Cut them out and form three piles of eight squares.

3 On the top squares, draw a circle ⁹⁄₁₆ in. (1.5 cm) in diameter.

4 Hold a pile together between your fingers and cut out the circles. Repeat this for the other piles.

5 Run the back of your blade along the middle of the circle and then fold them in half.

6 Glue each half circle to another half until the fruit is closed.

7 Spread each slice apart to form a round fruit.

8 Repeat steps 6 and 7 twice to form the other two berries.

Berry

ASSEMBLING THE WREATH

1 Place all the elements on the circle (without gluing them), as shown in the photo.

2 With a glue gun, first attach the large anemone, then the ranunculus, and then the small white anemone. Press until they are secure.

3 Then glue the carnations by inserting the tips under the other flowers.

4 Glue on the berries and finish with the leaves by inserting them under the flowers.

INSTALLING THE WREATH

1 Cut a 7⅞ in. (20 cm) piece of string or ribbon.

2 Tie its two ends together.

3 Place your string under the circle by placing the loop near the circle.

4 Insert the knot into the loop and pull the end of the string.

5 Hang your wreath on a nail.

Tip: If you can't find a gold lampshade circle, spray one with gold paint.

LAURE FARION is the founder of the popular brand PapierPapierPapier, where thousands enjoy her imaginative paper-crafting ideas. Laure's degrees in design, architecture, and upholstery decor have helped forge her special bond with paper. She taught art for a while, then the desire to devote herself to creation led her to found her brand PapierPapierPapier. Laure creates paper art for corporate product design, creates ephemeral art installations of paper, and shares her joy in paper craft with a wide online audience.